PRACTICE MULTIPLE CHOICE QUESTIONS

CSEC®
Principles
of Accounts

**Lystra Stephens-James, Dyann Barras,
Carl Herrera, Kirk Philip**

William Collins' dream of knowledge for all began with the publication of his first book in 1819.
A self-educated mill worker, he not only enriched millions of lives, but also founded a flourishing publishing house.
Today, staying true to this spirit, Collins books are packed with inspiration, innovation and practical expertise. They place you at the centre of a world of possibility and give you exactly what you need to explore it.

Collins. Freedom to teach.

Published by Collins
An imprint of HarperCollins*Publishers*
The News Building
1 London Bridge Street
London
SE1 9GF

Browse the complete Collins Caribbean catalogue at
www.collins.co.uk/caribbeanschools

ISBN 978-0-00-826040-8

Practice Multiple Choice Questions: CSEC® Principles of Accounts is an independent publication and has not been authorised, sponsored or otherwise approved by CXC®.

CSEC® is a registered trademark of the Caribbean Examinations Council (CXC®).

British Library Cataloguing in Publication Data
A catalogue record for this publication is available from the British Library.

The publishers gratefully acknowledge the permission granted to reproduce the copyright material in this book. Every effort has been made to trace copyright holders and to obtain their permission for the use of copyright material. The publishers will gladly receive any information enabling them to rectify any error or omission at the first opportunity.

Authors: Lystra Stephens-James, Dyann Barras, Carl Herrera, Kirk Philip
Publisher: Elaine Higgleton
Commissioning editor: Tom Hardy
In-house project lead: Caroline Green
Project manager: Alissa McWhinnie, QBS Learning
Copy editor: Stephen Cashmore
Proofreader: Alta Bridges
Answer checker: Kay Hawkins
Production controller: Tina Paul
Illustrator: QBS Learning
Typesetter: QBS Learning
Cover designers: Kevin Robbins and Gordon MacGilp
Printed and bound by Grafica Veneta, SpA, Italy

MIX
Paper from
responsible sources
FSC™ C007454

FSC
www.fsc.org

This book is produced from independently certified FSC™ paper
to ensure responsible forest management.

For more information visit: www.harpercollins.co.uk/green

Contents

Structure of the CSEC® Principles of Accounts Paper 1 Examination

There are 327 questions in the examination. The duration of each examination is **1 ½ hours**. The papers are worth **30%** of your final examination mark.

The Paper 1 examination test the following core areas of the syllabus.

Section	Number of Questions
1. Accounting as a profession	16
2. Accounting as a system	26
3. Books of original entry	30
4. Ledgers and the trial balance	35
5. The preparation and analysis of financial statements of the sole-trader	37
6. Accounting adjustments	35
7. Control systems	25
8. Accounting for partnerships	25
9. Accounting for limited liability companies, co-operatives and non-profit organisations	50
10. Manufacturing and inventory control	20
11. Accounting for the entrepreneur	28
Total Questions	**327**

Each question is allocated 1 mark. You will not lose a mark if a question is answered incorrectly.

Examination Tips

General strategies for answering multiple choice questions:

- Read every word of each question very carefully and make sure you understand exactly what it is asking. Even if you think that the question appears simple or straightforward there may be important information you could easily omit.

- When faced with a question that seems unfamiliar, re-read it very carefully. Underline or circle the key pieces of information provided. Re-read it again if necessary to make sure you are very clear as to what it is asking and that you are not misinterpreting it.

- Each question has four options, A, B, C and D, and only one is the correct answer. Look at all the options very carefully as the differences between them may be very subtle; never stop when you come across an option you think is the one required. Cross out options that you know are incorrect for certain. There may be two options that appear very similar; identify the difference between the two so you can select the correct answer.

- You have approximately 1 ½ minutes per question. Some questions can be answered in less time while other questions may require longer because of the reasoning or calculation involved. Do not spend too long on any one question.
- If a question appears difficult place a mark, such as an asterisk, on your answer sheet alongside the question number and return to it when you have finished answering all the other questions.
- Answer every question. Marks are not deducted for incorrect answers. Therefore, it is in your best interest to make an educated guess in instances where you do not know the answer. Never leave a question unanswered.
- Always ensure that you are shading the correct question number on your answer sheet. It is very easy to make a mistake, especially if you plan on returning to skipped questions.
- Some questions may ask which of the options is NOT correct or is INCORRECT. Pay close attention to this because it is easy to fail to see the words NOT or INCORRECT and answer the question incorrectly.
- Some questions may give two or more answers that could be correct and you are asked to determine which is the BEST or MOST LIKELY. You must consider each answer very carefully before making your choice because the differences between them may be very subtle.
- When a question gives three answers numbered I, II, III, one or more of these answers may be correct. You will then be given four combinations as options, for example:

  (A) I only   **(B)** I and II   **(C)** I and III or II and III   **(D)** I, II and III

  Place a tick by all the answers that you think are correct before you decide on the final correct combination.
- Do not make any assumptions about your choice of options; just because two answers in succession have been C, it does not mean that the next one cannot be C as well.
- Phrases or options may be provided to match scenarios that may relate to more than one question. Place a tick by all answers you think are correct before you decide on the final option for each question.
- Try to leave time at the end of the examination to check over your answers, but never change an answer until you have thought about it again very carefully.
- If your country has already adopted doing CXC® multiple choice questions online, please remember to scroll back to incomplete questions and ensure that you have clicked on the correct answer.

Strategies for the CSEC® Principles of Accounts Paper 1:

- A silent, non-programmable calculator is allowed in the examination. You are required to carry your own calculator. Since different brands of calculators have unique features it is advisable to take a calculator you are familiar with.
- Be careful and accurate when performing calculations. It is very easy to make an error and there may be an incorrect option similar to your calculation. For questions requiring you to perform a calculation, work out the answer before you look at the four options. Do this by writing your working on the question paper. If you do not find your answer in the options, you can then go back and recheck your working for mistakes.
- Keep track of all units during calculations. The final unit in the result is a good clue if the calculation was done correctly.
- Some questions are accompanied by diagrams, graphs, table or prose. Read and inspect these carefully and use them to derive the best option for the question. You may make your own sketches to help you answer the questions.

1 Accounting is

(A) recording anything that happens in a business. ⒶA

(B) recording the transactions of a business. ⒷB

(C) recording, analysing and interpreting the business' transactions. ⒸC

(D) recording, summarising, analysing and interpreting the business' transactions. ⒹD

2 The recording of the transactions in the accounting books of a business is called

(A) accounting. ⒶA

(B) book-keeping. ⒷB

(C) liabilities. ⒸC

(D) resources. ⒹD

3 The purposes of preparing accounting documents and financial statements are to

I show information of the resources of a business.

II show who has claims on the business' resources.

III help users of financial information make decisions about the business.

(A) I and II ⒶA

(B) I and III ⒷB

(C) II and III ⒸC

(D) I, II and III ⒹD

1.2 The users of accounting information

4 Which lists represents both internal and external users of financial statements?

(A) Banks, government and investors   Ⓐ

(B) Creditors, government and managers   Ⓑ

(C) Creditors, banks and investors   Ⓒ

(D) Suppliers, investors and banks   Ⓓ

5 Which accounting user is correctly matched with its need?

(A) Banker – to determine taxes to charge the business   Ⓐ

(B) Government – to find out if the business can repay a loan   Ⓑ

(C) Supplier – to find out if he should invest capital in the business   Ⓒ

(D) Owner – to determine the profit of the business over the financial period   Ⓓ

6 Which of the following statements is NOT a need of a user of accounting information?

(A) To determine whether to invest further   Ⓐ

(B) To determine the profitability of the business   Ⓑ

(C) To find out the number of owners in the business   Ⓒ

(D) To add to the country's Gross Domestic Product (GDP)   Ⓓ

1.3 Traditional and emerging careers in the field of accounting

7 Why is accounting necessary in an organisation?

(A) It is required by law   Ⓐ

(B) To help the government   Ⓑ

(C) To report on financial data   Ⓒ

(D) To have enough employees   Ⓓ

8 In which of the following industries can people who are trained and skilled in accounting be employed?

> **I** Banking
>
> **II** Insurance
>
> **III** Construction

(A) I and II ⓐ

(B) I and III ⓑ

(C) II and III ⓒ

(D) I, II and III ⓓ

1.4 Ethical issues in the field of accounting

9 Marlon Ettienne prepared the financial statement for BrownTown Hardware. He is of the view that the statements should show more information about the transactions that are important to the owners than simply following accounting principles. His view is against the ethical principle in accounting of

(A) integrity. ⓐ

(B) objectivity. ⓑ

(C) confidentiality. ⓒ

(D) professional competence. ⓓ

10 Gordon Corbin, the manager of See Sea Hotel, fired his accountant. He then promoted his niece, Janet Cain, the bartender, who has no accounting training or experience, as the accountant. Which of the following does Janet lack?

(A) Integrity ⓐ

(B) Objectivity ⓑ

(C) Confidentiality ⓒ

(D) Professional competence ⓓ

11 Salina is newly employed as a clerk in the accounts department of Zanny Stores. She shared with her friend, the messenger, the balances in the three bank accounts of the business. Which ethical principle in accounting has she breached?

(A) Integrity   Ⓐ

(B) Objectivity   Ⓑ

(C) Confidentiality   Ⓒ

(D) Professional competence   Ⓓ

12 Allan Piper prepared a cheque for \$100 000 in his name and forged signatures on the cheque. Which of the following has Allan displayed a lack of?

(A) Integrity   Ⓐ

(B) Objectivity   Ⓑ

(C) Confidentiality   Ⓒ

(D) Professional competence   Ⓓ

13 John Dough, the accountant, does not lock unused cheques away securely, leaves cheques on his desk incomplete and accessible by other employees, and prepares reports two months after the month has passed. Which of the following describes John's behaviour?

(A) Lack of objectivity   Ⓐ

(B) Lack of confidentiality   Ⓑ

(C) Unprofessional behaviour   Ⓒ

(D) Unprofessional competence   Ⓓ

14 Applying accounting principles appropriately leads to

    I no errors being recorded in the information.

    II correct calculation of financial information.

    III the true nature of the transaction being reported.

(A) I and II   Ⓐ

(B) I and III   Ⓑ

(C) II and III   Ⓒ

(D) I, II and III   Ⓓ

15 A cashier at a leading private high school, responsible for collecting school fees from students, uses the fees from time to time to loan to employees, charging the employees 10% of the loan. The cashier hopes the employees repay quickly so that the missing funds will not be noticed. Some of the employees have not been repaying the loans and the manager has now asked the cashier to account for the shortages in the cash. Which of the following has the cashier been committing?

(A) Fraud   Ⓐ

(B) Tax evasion   Ⓑ

(C) Theft   Ⓒ

(D) Errors   Ⓓ

16 An employee that commits fraud or practices any other inappropriate application of accounting principles, may be

    I fired.

    II fined.

    III imprisoned.

(A) I and II   Ⓐ

(B) I and III   Ⓑ

(C) II and III   Ⓒ

(D) I, II and III   Ⓓ

Section 2: Accounting as a system
2.1 Concepts and conventions

1 Which of the following ensures that accountants use the same principles and methods of recording from year to year within a company?

(A) Accrual   Ⓐ

(B) Prudence   Ⓑ

(C) Consistency   Ⓒ

(D) Separate entity   Ⓓ

2 A business which switches its stock valuation method regularly is violating the accounting principle of

(A) double entry. (A)

(B) consistency. (B)

(C) business entity. (C)

(D) prudence. (D)

2.2 The accounting cycle

3 Which of the following stages of the accounting cycle is correct?

(A) Journalising, posting to the ledger, trial balance, financial statements (A)

(B) Posting to the ledger, journalising, trial balance, financial statements (B)

(C) Posting to the ledger, trial balance, financial statement, journalising (C)

(D) Trial balance, financial statements, posting to the ledger, journalising (D)

2.3 Business organisations

4 Which of the following are business organisations formed by members?

    I Cooperatives

    II Non-profit organisations

    III Partnerships

(A) I (A)

(B) II (B)

(C) I and II (C)

(D) I and III (D)

5 BLT Limited's Board raised its funds through the stock exchange. Which of the following is this activity a feature of?

(A) Partnership   Ⓐ

(B) Non-trading organisation   Ⓑ

(C) Corporation   Ⓒ

(D) Cooperative Society Limited   Ⓓ

2.4 The financial statements of business organisations

6 In which of the following are a sole trader's profits and losses recorded?

(A) Income Statement   Ⓐ

(B) Income and Expenditure Account   Ⓑ

(C) Balance Sheet   Ⓒ

(D) Cash Flow Statement   Ⓓ

7 Which of the following are financial reports of a Cooperative Society Limited?

    I Income and Expenditure Account

    II Balance Sheet

    III Income Statement

(A) I and II   Ⓐ

(B) I and III   Ⓑ

(C) II and III   Ⓒ

(D) I, II and III   Ⓓ

8 Which of the following statements reports on a business' cash receipts and cash payments for a specified period?

(A) Income Statement   Ⓐ

(B) Income and Expenditure   Ⓑ

(C) Balance Sheet   Ⓒ

(D) Cash Flow Statement   Ⓓ

9 Which of the following is NOT an advantage of a computerised accounting system?

(A) High installation and security costs (A)

(B) Greater storage of accounting information (B)

(C) Less time spent in accessing and retrieving data (C)

(D) Quicker access to accounting information and financial reports (D)

10 Computer software can be described as

    I instructions prepared by people.

    II packages embedded in programs.

    III devices stored in the hardware of a computer.

(A) I (A)

(B) II (B)

(C) I and II (C)

(D) I and III (D)

11 Which of the following accounting processes would MOST LIKELY NOT be used in a computerised accounting system?

(A) Payroll (A)

(B) Inventory control (B)

(C) Receivable schedule (C)

(D) Signing of cheques (D)

Item 12 refers to Kaleb's assets and liabilities, shown in the table.

	$
Cash in hand	500
Accounts payable	2 500
Bank overdraft	3 000
Accounts receivable	5 000
Premises	70 000
Cash at bank	5 000

12 Kaleb's capital amount is

(A) $75 000   Ⓐ

(B) $80 500   Ⓑ

(C) $81 000   Ⓒ

(D) $86 000   Ⓓ

13 It is the end of Tiffany's financial year. She had total assets of $5 000 and capital of $3 600. How much were her liabilities?

(A) $1 400   Ⓐ

(B) $3 600   Ⓑ

(C) $5 000   Ⓒ

(D) $8 600   Ⓓ

14 Under which of the following would Cash be classified in a Balance Sheet?

(A) Current Assets ⒶA

(B) Current Liabilities ⒷB

(C) Non-current Assets ⒸC

(D) Non-current Liabilities ⒹD

15 Under which of the following headings would Accounts Receivable be entered in the Balance Sheet?

(A) Capital ⒶA

(B) Fixed Assets ⒷB

(C) Current Assets ⒸC

(D) Current Liabilities ⒹD

16 Which of the following would be entered in the liabilities section of the Balance Sheet?

(A) Capital, accounts payable, cash ⒶA

(B) Cash, cash at bank, accounts payable ⒷB

(C) Accounts payable, bank overdraft, loan ⒸC

(D) Capital, cash, accounts payable ⒹD

17 Resources owned by the business are known as

(A) assets. ⒶA

(B) capital. ⒷB

(C) expenses. ⒸC

(D) liabilities. ⒹD

18 Mortgage and a five-year bank loan are classified in the Balance Sheet as

(A) current assets.   (A)

(B) current liabilities.   (B)

(C) non-current assets.   (C)

(D) non-current liabilities.   (D)

2.8 Types of assets and liabilities

Items 19 and 20 refer to the following balance sheet.

Assets	$	$
Land		80 000
Furniture		5 000
Motor vehicles		10 000
Machinery		20 000
Inventory		7 000
Accounts receivable		1 000
Cash at bank		7 000
Cash in hand		1 000
		131 000
Capital		
At start	100 000	
Add net profit:	28 000	
	128 000	
Less drawings:	(8 000)	
		120 000
Liabilities		
Creditors		3 000
Bank overdraft		8 000
		131 000

19 The value of the total current assets is

(A) $16 000   Ⓐ

(B) $21 000   Ⓑ

(C) $110 000   Ⓒ

(D) $115 000   Ⓓ

20 The total value of the non-current assets (fixed assets) is

(A) $ 16 000   Ⓐ

(B) $115 000   Ⓑ

(C) $120 000   Ⓒ

(D) $131 000   Ⓓ

21 Which of the following is a typical example of a non-current (long-term) liability?

(A) Mortgage   Ⓐ

(B) Accounts payable   Ⓑ

(C) Accounts receivable   Ⓒ

(D) Factory building   Ⓓ

2.9 Construction of a balance sheet

22 Which group of assets below is recorded in the 'Order of Permanence'?

(A) Cash, bank, accounts receivable, inventory   Ⓐ

(B) Accounts receivable, cash, bank, inventory   Ⓑ

(C) Inventory, bank, accounts receivable, cash   Ⓒ

(D) Inventory, accounts receivable, bank, cash   Ⓓ

23 The following lists of assets were found in Ashley's Balance Sheet. If they were to be arranged in the 'Order of Liquidity', the sequence would be

(A) building, land, cash, bank.   Ⓐ

(B) bank, cash, building, land.   Ⓑ

(C) cash, bank, building, land.   Ⓒ

(D) land, bank, building, cash.   Ⓓ

Items 24 and 25 refer to the following Balance Sheet information.

Salim

Balance Sheet as at 1 January 2017

	$	$
Inventory	6 000	
Accounts Receivable	I	
Cash at Bank	3 000	11 000
		11 000
II		9 000
Capital		2 000
		11 000

24 What sum of money is represented by **I** above?

(A) $2 000   Ⓐ

(B) $4 000   Ⓑ

(C) $11 000   Ⓒ

(D) $16 000   Ⓓ

25 Which of the following BEST describe **II** above?

(A) Total Assets   Ⓐ

(B) Total Capital   Ⓑ

(C) Total Expenses   Ⓒ

(D) Total Liabilities   Ⓓ

2.10 Changes in the balance sheet

26 How would the purchase of buildings on credit affect a firm's Balance Sheet?

(A) Increase assets; decrease liabilities　　　Ⓐ

(B) Decrease assets; decrease liabilities　　　Ⓑ

(C) Increase assets; increase liabilities　　　Ⓒ

(D) Decrease assets; increase liabilities　　　Ⓓ

Section 3: Books of original entry
3.1 Using books of original entry

1 Keri Walters, a sole trader, sold an old computer no longer suited to her business on credit. In which journal should Keri record her transaction?

(A) General Journal　　　Ⓐ

(B) Sales Journal　　　Ⓑ

(C) Sales Returns Journal　　　Ⓒ

(D) Petty Cash Book　　　Ⓓ

2 Which of the following are entries made in the Purchases Journal?

　　I Bought goods on credit

　　II Vehicle purchased on credit

　　III Goods bought on credit that have been undercharged

(A) I only　　　Ⓐ

(B) I and II only　　　Ⓑ

(C) I and III only　　　Ⓒ

(D) II and III only　　　Ⓓ

3 The total of inventory sent back by credit customers is recorded in which book?

(A) Sales Day Book   Ⓐ

(B) Purchases Day Book   Ⓑ

(C) Sales Returns Day Book   Ⓒ

(D) Purchases Returns Day Book   Ⓓ

4 The total value of goods sent back to credit suppliers is recorded in which book?

(A) Sales Day Book   Ⓐ

(B) Purchases Day Book   Ⓑ

(C) Sales Returns Day Book   Ⓒ

(D) Purchases Returns Day Book   Ⓓ

3.2 Cash and credit transactions

5 In which book of original entry should the business record a cheque sent to N. Rampersad for goods purchased?

(A) Purchases Day Book   Ⓐ

(B) Sales Day Book   Ⓑ

(C) General Journal   Ⓒ

(D) Cash Book   Ⓓ

6 Which of the following transactions should be debited in the Cash Book?

(A) Payment received from debtors   Ⓐ

(B) Goods sold on credit   Ⓑ

(C) Payment made for goods purchased   Ⓒ

(D) Goods bought for cash   Ⓓ

7 After a business sold goods on credit to Ann Wilson it was discovered that she was undercharged. Which of the following documents should be issued to her?

(A) Invoice   Ⓐ

(B) Credit note   Ⓑ

(C) Debit note   Ⓒ

(D) Advice note   Ⓓ

8 Details from which of the following are used to prepare the Petty Cash Book?

(A) Vouchers   Ⓐ

(B) Cheques   Ⓑ

(C) Invoices   Ⓒ

(D) Receipts   Ⓓ

Items 9 and 10 refer to the following information.

Philip Leslie, a customer, returned some goods previously purchased. They were the wrong colour.

9 In which book of original entry will this transaction be recorded?

(A) Purchases Journal   Ⓐ

(B) Customers' Return Journal   Ⓑ

(C) Returns Inwards Journal   Ⓒ

(D) Returns Outwards Journal   Ⓓ

10 What source document should be issued to Mr. Leslie?

(A) Invoice   Ⓐ

(B) Voucher   Ⓑ

(C) Debit note   Ⓒ

(D) Credit note   Ⓓ

11 The terms stated on an invoice were 5/14, n/30. This means that the customer is entitled to

(A) 30% if paid between 5–14 days. Ⓐ

(B) 5% if paid in 14 days. Ⓑ

(C) 14% if paid in 5 days. Ⓒ

(D) nothing down for 30 days. Ⓓ

Items 12 and 13 refer to the following Credit Note.

CREDIT NOTE

Kwesi Car Supplies Ltd

Omega Drive

To: Josiah Auto   No. 10030

                                             7 July, 2018

Item	Quantity	Unit Price $	Amount $
Engine Seals	125	50	6 250
Wiper Blades	24	20	480

---

12 In which of Kwesi Car Supplies Ltd books of original entry should the transaction be recorded?

(A) Sales Journal Ⓐ

(B) Purchases Journal Ⓑ

(C) Sales Returns Journal Ⓒ

(D) Purchases Returns Journal Ⓓ

13 Which of the following statements BEST describes the transaction which gave rise to the above document?

(A) Kwesi Car Supplies Ltd returned goods to Josiah Ltd   (A)

(B) Josiah Auto returned goods to Kwesi Car Supplies Ltd   (B)

(C) Kwesi Car Supplies Ltd purchased goods from Josiah Auto   (C)

(D) Josiah Auto purchased goods from Kwesi Car Supplies Ltd   (D)

3.6 Using source documents to complete books of original entry

14 In which of the following does a business record the details of an invoice sent to a customer?

(A) Cash Book   (A)

(B) Sales Journal   (B)

(C) General Journal   (C)

(D) Purchases Journal   (D)

15 In which of the following does a business record the details of a credit note received?

(A) Sales Journal   (A)

(B) Purchases Returns Journal   (B)

(C) Sales Return Journal   (C)

(D) Purchases Journal   (D)

16 Which of the following is NOT a contra entry?

(A) Deposited cash into bank   (A)

(B) Cashed cheque for office till   (B)

(C) Withdrew cash from bank for office use   (C)

(D) Cash sales paid directly into bank   (D)

17 Which of the following are contra entries?

     I Dr Cash; Cr Bank

     II Dr Bank; Cr Cash

     III Dr Cash; Cr Cash

(A) I and II   (A)

(B) I and III   (B)

(C) II and III   (C)

(D) I, II and III   (D)

Items 18 and 19 refer to the following incomplete invoice.

Garnet Grocery

Main Road

Spring Village

Sold To: Kyle Confectionery   Invoice No. 0501

                                              4 November 2018

Item	Quantity	Unit Price	Amount ($)
Sugar	20 bags	$20	400
Chocolate	50 lbs.	$15	750

Sale is subject to 6% trade discount

---

18 In the books of Kyle Confectionery, the above invoice would be recorded in the

(A) Cash Book.   (A)

(B) Sales Journal.   (B)

(C) General Journal.   (C)

(D) Purchases Journal.   (D)

19 The amount to be entered in the journal is

(A) $1 081. Ⓐ

(B) $1 150. Ⓑ

(C) $1 219. Ⓒ

(D) $2 450. Ⓓ

3.7 Trade and cash discounts

Items 20–22 refer to the following information.

Mr. Clunis bought goods on credit with a total list price of $1 800 less 10% trade discount. He is entitled to a further 5% cash discount if he settles his account in 30 days.

20 What amount would Mr. Clunis record in his Purchases Journal?

(A) $1 530 Ⓐ

(B) $1 539 Ⓑ

(C) $1 620 Ⓒ

(D) $1 800 Ⓓ

21 The amount of the trade discount is

(A) $90 Ⓐ

(B) $180 Ⓑ

(C) $190 Ⓒ

(D) $270 Ⓓ

22 What amount would Mr. Clunis pay if he settles his account in 30 days?

(A) $81 Ⓐ

(B) $1 539 Ⓑ

(C) $1 620 Ⓒ

(D) $1 800 Ⓓ

23 CAP Ltd paid Wright Enterprises $2 910 after deducting a 3% discount. The value of the discount was

(A) $90.00.   (A)

(B) $87.30.   (B)

(C) $30.00.   (C)

(D) $29.10.   (D)

24 Mr. Gary settled his account of $3 250 with Stapler Inc. by cheque and was allowed $50 off for early payment. How should the $50 be entered in Mr. Gary's cashbook?

(A) Discount allowed column on debit side   (A)

(B) Discount received column on credit side   (B)

(C) Discount received column on debit side   (C)

(D) Discount allowed column on credit side   (D)

3.9 Balancing cash books

Items 25 and 26 refer to the information in the following table.

	$
Petty cash balance b/d	30
To restore imprest at start	170
Petty cash expenses	110

25 What is the balance c/d at the end of the period?

(A) $30   (A)

(B) $90   (B)

(C) $110   (C)

(D) $170   (D)

26 How much will be needed to restore the imprest at the end of the period?

(A) $310   (A)

(B) $200   (B)

(C) $170   (C)

(D) $110   (D)

3.10 Interpreting cash book balances

27 A credit bank balance in the Cash Book indicates that

(A) a loss was made.   (A)

(B) a profit was made.   (B)

(C) the business had a surplus.   (C)

(D) the business used its overdraft.   (D)

3.11 Treatment of totals from books of original entry

28 The total of the Sales Return Journal will be posted to the respective account in which ledger?

(A) General Ledger   (A)

(B) Sales Ledger   (B)

(C) Returns Ledger   (C)

(D) Purchases Ledger   (D)

29 Where is the total of the Discount Received column in the Cash Book posted?

(A) Debit side discount received account   (A)

(B) Credit side discount received account   (B)

(C) Debit side discount allowed account   (C)

(D) Credit side discount allowed account   (D)

Item 30 refers to the following entry in the Returns Outwards Journal.

Returns Outwards Journal			
Date	**Details**	**Folio**	**Amount $**
March 14	N. Gomez	PL 16	168
March 18	W. Gittens	PL 40	109

30 What is the amount to be transferred to the Returns Outwards account?

(A) $59   Ⓐ

(B) $109   Ⓑ

(C) $168   Ⓒ

(D) $277   Ⓓ

Section 4: Ledgers and Trial Balance
4.1 Different classes of accounts

1 Which of the following accounts is NOT a real account?

(A) Land   Ⓐ

(B) Furniture   Ⓑ

(C) Motor vehicle   Ⓒ

(D) Motor vehicle repairs   Ⓓ

2 Nominal accounts include

    I Purchases and Sales

    II Motor car and Furniture

    III Carriage Inwards and Carriage Outwards

(A) I   Ⓐ

(B) I and II   Ⓑ

(C) I and III   Ⓒ

(D) II and III   Ⓓ

3 Which type of account is Building, Machinery and Office Equipment classified as?

(A) Real account   (A)

(B) Contra account   (B)

(C) Personal account   (C)

(D) Nominal account   (D)

4 Which class of account does Debtors and Creditors belong to?

(A) Real accounts   (A)

(B) Contra accounts   (B)

(C) Personal accounts   (C)

(D) Nominal accounts   (D)

4.2 Different types of ledger

5 You wish to make an entry in debtor Soomai's account. Select the option/s which is MOST closely related to it. Each option MAY be used more than once, or not at all.

(A) Cash book   (A)

(B) General ledger   (B)

(C) Purchases (accounts payable) ledger   (C)

(D) Sales (accounts receivable) ledger   (D)

6 You want to find records of expenses, capital and revenue (income accounts). Select the option/s which is MOST closely related to it. Each option MAY be used more than once, or not at all.

(A) Cash book   (A)

(B) General ledger   (B)

(C) Purchases (accounts receivable) ledger   (C)

(D) Sales (accounts receivable) ledger   (D)

7 Which of the following transactions should be credited in the bank account?

(A) Paid wages by cash (A)

(B) Received a loan from Shemeul (B)

(C) Sold goods and received a cheque (C)

(D) Bought goods and paid by cheque (D)

8 Which of the following double-entry rules apply to the owner contributing cash to the business?

    I Dr Assets

    II Cr Capital

    III Dr Liabilities

(A) I (A)

(B) II (B)

(C) I and II (C)

(D) II and III (D)

9 Makesi Soanes started a data processing company with $50 000 cash. Which of the following are accurate assumptions?

    I Increase asset and capital

    II Decrease asset and capital

    III Debit cash and credit capital

(A) I (A)

(B) II (B)

(C) I and II (C)

(D) I and III (D)

Item 10 refers to the following information.

Bank a/c				
2017	$			$
June 1	10 000			
3	20 000			
Vehicle a/c				
2017				
June 6	20 000			
Capital a/c				
		2017		
		June 1		10 000
		6		20 000
Bank Loan a/c				
		2017		
		June 3		20 000

10 The entries in the ledger accounts show that the business

    I started with money in the bank.

    II received a bank loan.

    III purchased a vehicle.

(A) I

(B) II

(C) I and II

(D) I and III

11 Ariel is a creditor of Moira and Malia (M & M) Ltd. The business settles a debt of $500 less 5% discount by cash. The entry to record this transaction in the books of M & M Ltd is

(A)

	Dr $	Cr $
Ariel	475	
Discount allowed	25	
Cash		500

Ⓐ

(B)

	Dr $	Cr $
Ariel	475	
Discount received	25	
Cash		500

Ⓑ

(C)

	Dr $	Cr $
Ariel	500	
Discount received		25
Cash		475

Ⓒ

(D)

	Dr $	Cr $
Cash	475	
Discount received	25	
Ariel		500

Ⓓ

12 Tia Marie purchased office equipment on credit from Raebekah for $4 000. The entry to record this transaction in Tia Marie's books is

(A)

	Dr $	Cr $
Equipment maintenance repairs	4 000	
Bank		4 000

(A)

(B)

	Dr $	Cr $
Purchases	4 000	
Accounts payable – Raebekah		4 000

(B)

(C)

	Dr $	Cr $
Equipment	4 000	
Bank		4 000

(C)

(D)

	Dr $	Cr $
Equipment	4 000	
Accounts payable – Raebekah		4 000

(D)

13 Keevan See, a sole trader, bought a new motor vehicle for $100 000. The business paid $10 000 in cash and traded in an old vehicle for the remainder. The entry to record this transaction is

(A)

	Dr $	Cr $
New motor vehicle	100 000	
Old motor vehicle		90 000
Cash		10 000

Ⓐ

(B)

	Dr $	Cr $
New motor vehicle	90 000	
Cash	10 000	
Old motor vehicle		100 000

Ⓑ

(C)

	Dr $	Cr $
New motor vehicle	10 000	
Cash	90 000	
Old motor vehicle		100 000

Ⓒ

(D)

	Dr $	Cr $
Old motor vehicle	90 000	
Cash	10 000	
New motor vehicle		100 000

Ⓓ

14 Ateeba More withdraws goods from his business for his own use. The double entry to record this is

(A) Dr Purchases   Cr Drawings   Ⓐ

(B) Dr Drawings   Cr Sales   Ⓑ

(C) Dr Cash   Cr Drawings   Ⓒ

(D) Dr Drawings   Cr Purchases   Ⓓ

15 Rachel Difference is a seamstress. She bought materials from Mikela Maharaj Textile Store and paid by cheque. The CORRECT double entry in Rachel's ledger is

    (A) Dr Purchases   Cr Bank   (A)

    (B) Dr Bank   Cr Purchases   (B)

    (C) Dr Bank   Cr Mikela Maharaj Textile Store   (C)

    (D) Dr Purchases   Cr Mikela Maharaj Textile Store   (D)

16 Kaleb Grant paid $400 by cheque for wages. This transaction was entered in the Cash Book and posted to another ledger. The CORRECT double entry to record this transaction is

    (A) Dr Bank   Cr Wages   (A)

    (B) Dr Wages   Cr Bank   (B)

    (C) Dr Kaleb Grant   Cr Bank   (C)

    (D) Dr Cash   Cr Wages   (D)

17 Salim Williams receives a cheque of $10 000 as commission. The entry to record this transaction in Salim's books is

    (A) Dr Bank   Cr Commission   (A)

    (B) Dr Commission   Cr Bank   (B)

    (C) Dr Bank   Cr Cash   (C)

    (D) Dr Cash   Cr Bank   (D)

18 Kimmy Sahatoo deposited a cheque received from Keevan. Which of the following entries would be made in Kimmy's books to record the cheque deposited?

    I Debit cash

    II Debit bank

    III Credit Keevan

    (A) I   (A)

    (B) I and II   (B)

    (C) I and III   (C)

    (D) II and III   (D)

4.5 Posting from books of original entry to ledger accounts

Item 19 refers to the information below.

Kaleb Grant prepared the Purchases Day Book for the month of June 2017 with the following information.

Kaleb Grant

Purchases Day Book

Date	Details	Folio	Invoice No.	Amount
2017				$
June 20	Rochard Liverpool			350.00
June 25	George Wales			250.00

19 How should Grant post this information in his ledger at the end of June 2017?

(A) Dr Rochard Liverpool $350   Ⓐ

     Cr Purchases $600

     Cr George Wales $250

(B) Dr Purchases $600   Ⓑ

     Cr Rochard Liverpool $350

     Cr George Wales $250

(C) Dr Rochard Liverpool $ 350   Ⓒ

     Dr George Wales $250

     Cr Purchases $600

(D) Dr Purchases $350   Ⓓ

     Cr George Wales $600

     Cr Rochard Liverpool $250

20 Credit notes received entered in a specific book of original entry will be posted in the general ledger to the

(A) Sales account. (A)

(B) Purchases account. (B)

(C) Purchases Returns account. (C)

(D) Sales Returns account. (D)

Items 21–22 refer to the following information.

Karissa's Cash Book

Date	Details	Dis. A	Cash	Bank	Date	Details	Dis. R	Cash	Bank
2017		$	$	$	2017		$	$	$
July 1	Bal. b/d		4 000	3 000	July 2	Tevon	80		1 620
July 18	Sherma	20		480					
Totals		20					80		

21 To which ledger would the totals of the discount columns be posted?

(A) Sales ledger (A)

(B) Purchases ledger (B)

(C) General ledger (C)

(D) Cash book (D)

22 To which ledger would the entry on July 18 be posted?

(A) Sales ledger (A)

(B) Purchases ledger (B)

(C) General ledger (C)

(D) Returns ledger (D)

23 The cash book has unique features that are different from other books of original entry. It functions as a

  I journal.

  II trial balance.

  III ledger account.

(A) I   (A)

(B) I and II   (B)

(C) I and III   (C)

(D) II and III   (D)

Item 24 refers to the following information.

Sheree

General Journal

Date	Details	Dr	Cr
2017		$	$
July 22	Equipment	15 600	
	Lesley Burrows		15 600

24 The entry for posting to the ledger is

(A) Dr Equipment   Cr Lesley Burrows   (A)

(B) Dr Cash   Cr Equipment   (B)

(C) Dr Lesley Burrows   Cr Equipment   (C)

(D) Dr Equipment   Cr Cash   (D)

25 The analysis columns' totals from the petty cash book are posted to the

    I General ledger.

    II Accounts Receivable ledger.

    III Accounts Payable ledger.

(A) I and II   Ⓐ

(B) I and III   Ⓑ

(C) II and III   Ⓒ

(D) I, II and III   Ⓓ

4.6 Balancing and closing accounts

Item 26 refers to the following information.

The following account was extracted from the Sales ledger.

Aaliyah Devulge a/c					
2017		**$**	**2017**		**$**
May-05	Sales	800	May-08	Cash	800
12	Sales	3 000	13	Bank	2 500
15	Sales	2 000	13	Discount Allowed	300
			18	Bank	1 500

26 What is the closing balance?

(A) Debit balance b/d of $700   Ⓐ

(B) Credit balance b/d of $700   Ⓑ

(C) Debit balance b/d of $5 800   Ⓒ

(D) Credit balance b/d of $5 800   Ⓓ

Item 27 refers to the following information.

Cash a/c					
2017		**$**	**2017**		**$**
Jun-01	Balance b/d	10 000	Jun-05	Purchases	8 000
20	Sales	3 000	30	Wages	3 000

27 What is the closing balance of the cash account?

(A) $1 100   Ⓐ

(B) $1 300   Ⓑ

(C) $2 000   Ⓒ

(D) $3 000   Ⓓ

4.7 Interpreting entries and balances

28 Riaz sent an invoice to a customer for $8 000 less 25% trade discount. Later, the customer returned one-fifth (1/5) of the goods. What amount would be entered in his returns inwards account?

(A) $750   Ⓐ

(B) $1 200   Ⓑ

(C) $1 750   Ⓒ

(D) $2 000   Ⓓ

Item 29 refers to the following information.

A business uses the following steps to balance its individual ledger accounts.

    I The debit total and the credit total are drawn to be shown on the same line

    II Total both sides to determine which is greater

    III The balance is entered in the line below the total line

    IV Deduct the lesser side from the greater side

    V Enter the balance on the lesser side to make it equal

29 Which of the following is the correct sequence to balance the ledger accounts?

    (A) I, II III, IV, V   Ⓐ

    (B) III, I, II, IV, V   Ⓑ

    (C) IV, V, III, II, I   Ⓒ

    (D) II, IV, V, I, III   Ⓓ

30 Which of the accounts will ALWAYS have a debit balance?

    (A) Cash   Ⓐ

    (B) Bank   Ⓑ

    (C) Debtor   Ⓒ

    (D) Creditor   Ⓓ

31 Which of the following describes a ledger account with a balance brought down (b/d) on the debit side?

    (A) Asset   Ⓐ

    (B) Capital   Ⓑ

    (C) Income   Ⓒ

    (D) Liability   Ⓓ

Item 32 refers to the following information.

Bank a/c					
2017		**$**	**2017**		**$**
Jun-05	Sales	3 000	Jun-05	Opening balance	5 000
8	Sales	4 000	5	Furniture	3 000
30	Balance c/d		11	Salaries	2 000
		10 000			**10 000**

32 On which side of the Trial Balance will the CORRECT closing balance be shown?

(A) Dr $3 000

(B) Cr $3 000

(C) Dr $10 000

(D) Cr $10 000

(A)
(B)
(C)
(D)

33 Which of the following entries are NOT shown on the debit side of a Trial Balance?

(A) Purchases, Drawings, Cash

(B) Sales returns, Furniture and Fixtures, Office Equipment

(C) Purchases returns, Accounts Payable, Bank overdraft

(D) Accounts Receivable, Wages expense, Stock/Inventory

(A)
(B)
(C)
(D)

34 Which of the following accounts should be entered in the credit column of a Trial Balance?

(A) Drawings

(B) Cash in hand

(C) Accounts Receivable

(D) Bank overdraft

(A)
(B)
(C)
(D)

35 The listing prepared by accounts personnel to determine the arithmetical accuracy of double entry postings is known as the

(A) Trial Balance. (A)

(B) Balance Sheet. (B)

(C) Control Accounts. (C)

(D) Income Statement. (D)

Section 5: The preparation and analysis of financial statements of a sole trader
5.1 Purpose of preparing financial statements

1 What MAIN need of an owner is satisfied by the preparation of financial statements?

(A) Getting information included in the Gross Domestic Product (GDP) (A)

(B) Helping to decide whether to extend credit facilities (B)

(C) Helping to assess whether to negotiate for increased wages for employees (C)

(D) Determining if the business is profitable (D)

2 What needs of government are satisfied by the preparation of financial statements?

    I Gross Domestic Product (GDP) information

    II To provide assistance for firms

    III To assess taxes owed by the business

(A) I and II (A)

(B) I and III (B)

(C) II and III (C)

(D) I, II and III (D)

3 What category of user requires information about the business' ability to repay its short-term obligations?

(A) Debtors   Ⓐ

(B) Creditors   Ⓑ

(C) Government   Ⓒ

(D) Owners   Ⓓ

5.2 Components of financial statements

4 Which financial statement of a business shows the business' financial performance?

(A) Appropriation Account   Ⓐ

(B) Balance Sheet   Ⓑ

(C) Cash Flow Statement   Ⓒ

(D) Income Statement   Ⓓ

5 Which financial statement of a business shows the business' financial position?

(A) Appropriation Account   Ⓐ

(B) Balance Sheet   Ⓑ

(C) Cash Flow Statement   Ⓒ

(D) Income Statement   Ⓓ

5.3 Income statement for sole traders

6 Which of the following represents Opening Inventory added to Net Purchases?

(A) Cost of goods sold   Ⓐ

(B) Cost of goods available for sale   Ⓑ

(C) Gross profit   Ⓒ

(D) Total expenses   Ⓓ

7 What is the name of the figure from which closing inventory is subtracted?

(A) Opening Inventory   Ⓐ

(B) Net Purchases   Ⓑ

(C) Cost of Goods Available for Sale   Ⓒ

(D) Cost of Goods Sold   Ⓓ

8 Which of the following represents the figure obtained when Closing Inventory is deducted in the Income Statement?

(A) Net Sales   Ⓐ

(B) Cost of Goods Sold   Ⓑ

(C) Gross Profit   Ⓒ

(D) Net Income   Ⓓ

9 Another name for transportation on purchases is

(A) Carriage Inwards.   Ⓐ

(B) Carriage Outwards.   Ⓑ

(C) Returns Inwards.   Ⓒ

(D) Returns Outwards.   Ⓓ

10 Returns Inwards is

(A) added to Purchases.   Ⓐ

(B) subtracted from Purchases.   Ⓑ

(C) added to Sales.   Ⓒ

(D) subtracted from Sales.   Ⓓ

11 Returns Outwards is

(A) added to Purchases.   Ⓐ

(B) subtracted from Purchases.   Ⓑ

(C) added to Sales.   Ⓒ

(D) subtracted from Sales.   Ⓓ

12 Demerara Supermarket provides a delivery service to customers. The supermarket pays the drivers for delivering the groceries to the customers. What is this cost to Demerara Supermarket called?

(A) Carriage Outwards   Ⓐ

(B) Carriage Inwards   Ⓑ

(C) Returns Outwards   Ⓒ

(D) Returns Inwards   Ⓓ

13 Wages is listed as

(A) revenue in the Income Statement.   Ⓐ

(B) expense in the Income Statement.   Ⓑ

(C) a current asset in the Balance Sheet.   Ⓒ

(D) a current liability in the Balance Sheet.   Ⓓ

14 The salary for the delivery person employed by San Fernando Enterprises is listed as

(A) revenue in the Income Statement.   Ⓐ

(B) expense in the Income Statement.   Ⓑ

(C) a current asset in the Balance Sheet.   Ⓒ

(D) a current liability in the Balance Sheet.   Ⓓ

Items **15–17** refer to the following Income Statement.

Jonny Bake

Income Statement

for the year ended December 2017

Sales			60 000
I			(2 500)
Net Sales			57 500
		4 000	
Purchases		38 000	
Less: Returns Outwards		**II**	
		III	
Cost of Goods Available for Sale		37 500	
Less: Closing Inventory		(2 500)	
			(35 000)
Gross Profit			**IV**
Less: Total Expenses			(10 500)
Net Income			**V**

15 I represents which item in the above Income Statement?

(A) Cost of Sales   (A)

(B) Net Purchases   (B)

(C) Opening Inventory   (C)

(D) Returns Inwards   (D)

16 The value of **II** is

(A) $4 500.   (A)

(B) $12 000.   (B)

(C) $22 500.   (C)

(D) $33 500.   (D)

17 The value of **V** is

(A) $4 500. Ⓐ

(B) $12 000. Ⓑ

(C) $22 500. Ⓒ

(D) $33 500. Ⓓ

18 Which equation represents Gross Profit?

(A) Net Purchases – Net Sales Ⓐ

(B) Net Sales – Net Purchases Ⓑ

(C) Net Sales – cost of Goods Available for Sale Ⓒ

(D) Net Sales – cost of Sales Ⓓ

19 Which equation represents Net Income?

(A) Net Sales – Gross Profit Ⓐ

(B) Gross Profit – Cost of Goods Sold Ⓑ

(C) Gross Profit – Total Expenses Ⓒ

(D) Net Sales – Cost of Goods Sold Ⓓ

5.4 Classified Balance Sheet
5.5 Working capital

20 Motor Vehicles are listed as a

(A) Current Asset in the Balance Sheet. Ⓐ

(B) Current Liability in the Balance Sheet. Ⓑ

(C) Non-current Asset in the Balance Sheet. Ⓒ

(D) Non-current Liability in the Balance Sheet. Ⓓ

21 Creditors or Accounts Payable are listed as a

(A) Current Asset in the Balance Sheet. Ⓐ

(B) Current Liability in the Balance Sheet. Ⓑ

(C) Non-current Asset in the Balance Sheet. Ⓒ

(D) Non-current Liability in the Balance Sheet. Ⓓ

22 Short-term investments are listed as a

(A) Current Asset in the Balance Sheet. Ⓐ

(B) Current Liability in the Balance Sheet. Ⓑ

(C) Non-current Asset in the Balance Sheet. Ⓒ

(D) Non-current Liability in the Balance Sheet. Ⓓ

23 Bank overdraft is listed as a

(A) Current Asset in the Balance Sheet. Ⓐ

(B) Current Liability in the Balance Sheet. Ⓑ

(C) Non-current Asset in the Balance Sheet. Ⓒ

(D) Non-current Liability in the Balance Sheet. Ⓓ

24 Inventory is listed as a

(A) Current Asset in the Balance Sheet. Ⓐ

(B) Current Liability in the Balance Sheet. Ⓑ

(C) Non-current Asset in the Balance Sheet. Ⓒ

(D) Non-current Liability in the Balance Sheet. Ⓓ

Item 25 refers to the figures in the following table.

	$
Accounts receivable (Debtors)	7 000
Bank overdraft	2 000
Cash	500
Inventory	4 000
Accounts payable (Creditors)	4 500

25 What is the value of Working Capital?

(A) $0

(B) $1 000

(C) $5 000

(D) $9 000

Ⓐ

Ⓑ

Ⓒ

Ⓓ

5.6 Performance ratios

Items 26–28 refer to the following information.

M. Stuart, a sole trader, has a business named Caring Catering located in Sandy Point Town, St. Kitts. She provided the following information from the business' financial statements.

Opening Inventory	$8 600	Closing Inventory	$10 800
Net Sales	$65 000	Cost of Sales	$34 000
Gross Profit	$31 000	Net Profit Percentage	18%
Current Assets	$72 000	Current Liabilities	$48 000

26 What is the Stock Turnover / Inventory Turnover?

(A) 3.15 times

(B) 3.51 times

(C) 3.95 times

(D) 6.70 times

Ⓐ

Ⓑ

Ⓒ

Ⓓ

45

27 What is the value of the Gross Profit Percentage / Gross Margin?

(A) 43.06%

(B) 47.69%

(C) 64.58%

(D) 91.18%

28 What is the value of Net Profit / Net Income?

(A) $6 120

(B) $8 640

(C) $11 700

(D) $12 960

<u>Item 29</u> refers to the information in the following table.

	Firm A	Firm B
	$	$
Net Sales	10 000	15 000
Gross Profit	5 000	5 000
Net income	1 000	1 500

I Firm A has a greater gross profit percentage than Firm B

II Firm B has a greater gross profit percentage than Firm A

III Firm A and Firm B has the same net profit percentage

29 Which of the statements above are true?

(A) I and II

(B) I and III

(C) II and III

(D) I, II and III

Items 30 and 31 refers to the information in the following table.

	$		$
Inventory	10 000	Accounts Payable	15 000
Accounts Receivable	8 000	6 Months Loan	5 000
Cash	3 000	Bank	4 000
Mortgage	45 000	Equipment	26 000

30 Determine the value of the Current Ratio or Working Capital Ratio.

(A) 0.40 : 1

(B) 0.81 : 1

(C) 0.83 : 1

(D) 1.25 : 1

Ⓐ

Ⓑ

Ⓒ

Ⓓ

31 Determine the value of the Quick Ratio/Acid Test Ratio.

(A) 0.40 : 1

(B) 0.75 : 1

(C) 0.83 : 1

(D) 1.39 : 1

Ⓐ

Ⓑ

Ⓒ

Ⓓ

32 A current ratio of 2.5 : 1 means which of the following?

(A) Current liabilities are greater than current assets

(B) For every $1.00 of current assets the business has short-term debt of $2.50

(C) For every $1.00 of current liabilities the business has $2.50 of current assets

(D) The business should close because it is not able to pay its short-term debt

Ⓐ

Ⓑ

Ⓒ

Ⓓ

33 Terrel George started business with a retail store in Castries, St. Lucia, with a building worth $20 000 and cash of $8 000. At the end of the year he had an ending capital of $36 000 after making drawings during the year of $4 000. What is his **net income (net profit)** for the year?

(A) $4 000   Ⓐ

(B) $12 000   Ⓑ

(C) $28 000   Ⓒ

(D) $32 000   Ⓓ

Item 34 refers to the following information.

The following information is supplied from the business of Ms. Analise Hosam, a sole trader in St. Marys, Jamaica.

2016		$	2015		$
Jan-01	Capital at start	25 000	Dec-31	Capital at end	49 000
	Additional Capital invested	7 000		Drawings	3 500

34 What is the net income for the year?

(A) $13 500   Ⓐ

(B) $20 500   Ⓑ

(C) $34 500   Ⓒ

(D) $63 500   Ⓓ

Item 35 refers to the following information.

J. Sanchez, owner of the Fig Tree Restaurant in Fig Tree, Nevis, supplied the following balances.

Capital at 1 Sept. 2017 $45 000
Capital at 31 Aug. 2018 $39 000
Drawings $17 000

35 What is the net profit or loss for the accounting period?

(A) Net Loss $11 000   (A)

(B) Net Profit $11 000   (B)

(C) Net Profit $23 000   (C)

(D) Net Profit $67 000   (D)

5.9 Making recommendations based on ratio analysis

<u>Items 36 and 37</u> refer to the following information.

The Bank of Grand Bahama is evaluating four (4) sole traders to determine to which it should provide a loan of $100 000.

Name of Ratio	Firm A	Firm B	Firm C	Firm D
Current Ratio	3:1	1:1	1.6:1	2.5:1
Acid Test Ratio	1:1	0.98:1	1.5:1	1.3:1
Gross Profit Percentage	50%	40%	60%	55%
Net Profit Percentage	25%	15%	30%	30%

36 Which firm has the best ability to repay short-term obligations should creditors demand payment immediately?

(A) Firm A   (A)

(B) Firm B   (B)

(C) Firm C   (C)

(D) Firm D   (D)

37 Which firm seems to have the highest percentage of expenses?

(A) Firm A   (A)

(B) Firm B   (B)

(C) Firm C   (C)

(D) Firm D   (D)

Section 6: Accounting adjustments
6.1 Accounting concepts underpinning adjustments

Items 1–4 refer to the following table.

Commission Earned a/c			
Details	$	Details	$
		Bank	2 250
		Balance c/d	250

1 The amount of commission earned to be recorded in the Income Statement is

(A) $250. Ⓐ

(B) $2 000. Ⓑ

(C) $2 250. Ⓒ

(D) $2 500. Ⓓ

2 What does the balance of $250 represent?

(A) Prepaid expense Ⓐ

(B) Prepaid revenue Ⓑ

(C) Accrued expense Ⓒ

(D) Accrued revenue Ⓓ

3 The amount of $250 should be shown in the Balance Sheet under which of the following?

(A) Current Assets Ⓐ

(B) Current Liabilities Ⓑ

(C) Non-current Liabilities Ⓒ

(D) Owner's Equity Ⓓ

4 The accounting concept which guides the above account is known as the

(A) Prudence concept. Ⓐ

(B) Accruals concept. Ⓑ

(C) Consistency concept. Ⓒ

(D) Entity concept. Ⓓ

6.3 Journal entries and ledger accounts reflecting adjustments

Item 5 relates to the following table.

Electricity a/c		
	$	
Balance b/d	350	

5 What does the amount of $350 represent?

(A) An amount owing Ⓐ

(B) The expense for the period Ⓑ

(C) An amount paid in advance Ⓒ

(D) The amount paid for the period Ⓓ

6 A business recorded rent paid of $9 000 by cheque on 30 June. The accountant later stated that the payment was for three months ending 31 August. How will this adjustment be recorded on 30 June?

(A) Dr Bank $6 000; Cr Rent $6 000 Ⓐ

(B) Dr Prepaid Rent $6 000; Cr Rent $6 000 Ⓑ

(C) Dr Bank $6 000; Cr Profit and Loss $6 000 Ⓒ

(D) Dr Balance Sheet $6 000; Cr Rent $6 000 Ⓓ

7 Fortune Enterprises has a credit balance b/d of $750 on its Cable Expense account. This means that at the start of the period $750 was

(A) accrued.

(A)

(B) prepaid.

(B)

(C) paid.

(C)

(D) overpaid.

(D)

6.4 Bad debts

Items 8 and 9 refer to the following information.

A business has accumulated debtors since starting two years ago and has been advised to establish a provision for doubtful debts as follows:

Age of debtors	Amount	Percentage
17–24 months	$ 5 000	3%
9–16 months	$ 8 000	2%
1–8 months	$12 000	1%

8 The total of the provision for doubtful debts is

(A) $430.

(A)

(B) $500.

(B)

(C) $750.

(C)

(D) $1 500.

(D)

9 Which of the following accounting concepts governs the creation of a provision for doubtful debts?

(A) Accruals

(A)

(B) Consistency

(B)

(C) Double Entry

(C)

(D) Prudence

(D)

10 Amounts considered irrecoverable are referred to as

(A) bad debts.   (A)

(B) accrued expenses.   (B)

(C) depreciation.   (C)

(D) liabilities.   (D)

6.5 Journal entries and ledger accounts for bad and doubtful debts

11 A firm's accountant changed the Provision for Bad Debts from $500 to $350. What is the entry to record this decision?

(A) Dr Profit and Loss $500   Cr Provision for Bad Debts $500   (A)

(B) Dr Provision For Bad Debts $350   Cr Profit and Loss $350   (B)

(C) Dr Profit and Loss $150;   Cr Provision for Bad Debts $150   (C)

(D) Dr Provision for Bad Debts $150   Cr Profit and Loss $150   (D)

Items 12 and 13 refer to the following information.

A debtor owes $850 and is declared bankrupt. He is, however, able to pay $0.40 on every dollar owed.

12 How will his payment be recorded?

(A) Dr Cash $ 340   Cr Debtor $340   (A)

(B) Dr Cash $850   Cr Debtor $850   (B)

(C) Dr Debtor $340   Cr Cash $340   (C)

(D) Dr Debtor $850   Cr Cash $850   (D)

13 How will the bad debt be recorded?

(A) Dr Bad Debts $510	Cr Debtor $510	Ⓐ
(B) Dr Debtor $510	Cr Bad Debts $510	Ⓑ
(C) Dr Bad Debts $850	Cr Debtor $850	Ⓒ
(D) Dr Debtor $850	Cr Bad Debts $850	Ⓓ

14 What is the accounting entry to close off the bad debts a/c?

(A) Dr Bad Debts	Cr Income statement	Ⓐ
(B) Dr Income statement	Cr Bad Debts	Ⓑ
(C) Dr Balance Sheet	Cr Bad Debts	Ⓒ
(D) Dr Bad Debts	Cr Balance Sheet	Ⓓ

6.6 Bad and doubtful debts in the income statement and balance sheet

15 The provision for doubtful debts is deducted from which item in the Balance Sheet?

(A) Inventory   Ⓐ

(B) Owner's equity   Ⓑ

(C) Accounts payable   Ⓒ

(D) Accounts receivable   Ⓓ

Items 16 and 17 refer to the following information.

A firm has an existing provision for doubtful debts of $300. Debtors are currently $25 000 but the firm wishes to increase its provision for doubtful debts from 3% to 5%.

16 Which of the following entries is correct to record the provision for the current year?

(A)

Details	Dr	Cr
	$	$
Profit & Loss	500	
Provision for doubtful debts		500

Ⓐ

(B)

Details	Dr	Cr
	$	$
Provision for doubtful debts	750	
Profit & Loss		750

Ⓑ

(C)

Details	Dr	Cr
	$	$
Profit & Loss	950	
Provision for doubtful debts		950

Ⓒ

(D)

Details	Dr	Cr
	$	$
Provision for doubtful debts	1 250	
Profit & Loss		1 250

Ⓓ

17 The amount to be deducted from debtors in the Balance Sheet is

(A) $500. Ⓐ

(B) $750. Ⓑ

(C) $950. Ⓒ

(D) $1 250 Ⓓ

18 A computer was purchased on 1 January 2017 for $10 000. It is depreciated at a rate of 5% per annum using the diminishing balance method. What will be the depreciation charge for the year ending 31 December 2018?

(A) $475   Ⓐ

(B) $500   Ⓑ

(C) $950   Ⓒ

(D) $1 000   Ⓓ

Item 19 refers to the following information.

Equipment at cost	$21 800
Provision for depreciation	$9 810
Depreciation method	15% straight line

19 What is the annual depreciation amount?

(A) $1 472   Ⓐ

(B) $3 270   Ⓑ

(C) $9 810   Ⓒ

(D) $13 080   Ⓓ

Items 20 and 21 refer to the following information.

The following is the calculation for depreciation using the straight line method:

$$\frac{12\,000 - 1\,500}{5}$$

20 The annual depreciation is

(A) $1 500.   Ⓐ

(B) $2 100.   Ⓑ

(C) $7 500.   Ⓒ

(D) $12 000.   Ⓓ

21 In the above formula the value $1 500 represents the

   (A) cost price.   Ⓐ

   (B) net book value.   Ⓑ

   (C) disposal value.   Ⓒ

   (D) accumulated depreciation.   Ⓓ

Items 22–25 refer to the information in the following table.

Balance Sheet (Extract) as at 31 March 2019	
Fixed Assets	$
Land and Building	240 000
Less: Provision for depreciation*	(45 600)

* Depreciation is charged at a rate of 10% using the reducing balance method.

22 What is the current value of accumulated depreciation?

   (A) $4 560   Ⓐ

   (B) $24 000   Ⓑ

   (C) $45 600   Ⓒ

   (D) $48 000   Ⓓ

23 The net book value is

   (A) $45 600.   Ⓐ

   (B) $194 400.   Ⓑ

   (C) $240 000.   Ⓒ

   (D) $285 600.   Ⓓ

24 What would be the depreciation charge for 2020?

(A) $19 440

(B) $24 000

(C) $45 600

(D) $69 600

    Ⓐ

    Ⓑ

    Ⓒ

    Ⓓ

25 What would be the age of the asset at the end of year 2020?

(A) 2 years

(B) 3 years

(C) 4 years

(D) 5 years

    Ⓐ

    Ⓑ

    Ⓒ

    Ⓓ

6.9 Journal entries and ledger accounts for depreciation

26 The double entry to record depreciation is

(A) Dr Profit and Loss	Cr Balance Sheet	Ⓐ
(B) Dr Balance Sheet	Cr Profit and Loss	Ⓑ
(C) Dr Provision for depreciation	Cr Profit and Loss	Ⓒ
(D) Dr Profit and Loss	Cr Provision for depreciation	Ⓓ

27 Which of the following formulae BEST describes 'net book value'?

(A) Cost – Depreciation

(B) Cost – Accumulated Depreciation

(C) Cost – Disposal Value

(D) Cost + Provision for depreciation

    Ⓐ

    Ⓑ

    Ⓒ

    Ⓓ

Items 28 and 29 refer to the following information.

	$
Purchase of equipment	20 000
Delivery of equipment	500
Installation of equipment	2 000
Maintenance of equipment	1 250
Wages	3 750
Electricity	2 150

28 The total value of capital expenditure is

(A) $29 650   Ⓐ

(B) $23 750   Ⓑ

(C) $22 500   Ⓒ

(D) $20 000   Ⓓ

29 The total value of revenue expenditure is

(A) $5 900   Ⓐ

(B) $7 150   Ⓑ

(C) $7 650   Ⓒ

(D) $9 650   Ⓓ

30 Which of the following are methods used to calculate depreciation?

    I Net Book Value

    II Straight Line

    III Declining Balance

(A) I and II   Ⓐ

(B) I and III   Ⓑ

(C) II and III   Ⓒ

(D) I, II and III   Ⓓ

Items 31 and 32 refer to the information in the following table.

Motor Expense a/c			
Details	$	Details	$
Cash	5 000	Balance b/d	2 500
		Balance c/d	1 000

31 The amount to be transferred to the Income Statement is

(A) $1 000.   Ⓐ

(B) $1 500.   Ⓑ

(C) $5 000.   Ⓒ

(D) $8 500.   Ⓓ

32 The balance c/d of $1 000 represents

(A) an outstanding amount.   Ⓐ

(B) a prepaid amount.   Ⓑ

(C) the expense for the period.   Ⓒ

(D) the payment for the period.   Ⓓ

33 Under which balance sheet item will prepaid rent revenue appear?

(A) Current Assets   Ⓐ

(B) Current Liabilities   Ⓑ

(C) Working Capital   Ⓒ

(D) Owner's Equity   Ⓓ

6.13 Preparing financial statements after adjustments

<u>Items 34 and 35</u> refer to the following information.

A business paid an insurance premium of $1 800 on 1 June. The payment was for a three-month period.

34 What is the amount of the expense to be recorded in Income Statement for the second month?

(A) $600   Ⓐ

(B) $1 200   Ⓑ

(C) $1 800   Ⓒ

(D) $3 600   Ⓓ

35 At the end of the second month, which of the following will the Balance Sheet reflect?

(A) Prepayment of $600   Ⓐ

(B) Accrual of $600   Ⓑ

(C) Prepayment of $1 200   Ⓒ

(D) Accrual of $1 200   Ⓓ

Section 7: Control systems

7.1 Uses of control systems in the accounting process

1 Firms have control systems to:

    I protect its assets

    II reduce accounting errors

    III improve the reliability of financial information

(A) I and II   (A)

(B) I and III   (B)

(C) II and III   (C)

(D) I, II and III   (D)

7.2 Commonly used control systems in the accounting process

2 In an accounting process, there are common tools that a firm can use in its control systems. Which of the following systems locate subsidiary ledgers errors?

(A) Control accounts   (A)

(B) Trial balance   (B)

(C) Income Statement   (C)

(D) Bank reconciliation statement   (D)

3 Salim posted goods purchased from Bernard in Justin's account. What kind of error is this?

(A) Error of commission Ⓐ

(B) Error of principle Ⓑ

(C) Error of original entry Ⓒ

(D) Complete reversal of entries Ⓓ

4 Zari forgot to record a cheque payment of $5 000 for goods sold to a customer. What kind of error is this?

(A) Error of commission Ⓐ

(B) Error of omission Ⓑ

(C) Error of original entry Ⓒ

(D) Complete reversal of entries Ⓓ

5 Riaz Chamberlain overlooked an invoice from a supplier, Shemuel Gowrie. What type of error is this?

(A) Error of original entry Ⓐ

(B) Error of commission Ⓑ

(C) Complete reversal of entries Ⓒ

(D) Error of omission Ⓓ

6 A cheque for $750 paid for interest charges was posted to the accounts in error for $705. What type of error is this?

(A) Error of commission Ⓐ

(B) Error of original entry Ⓑ

(C) Compensating errors Ⓒ

(D) Complete reversal of entries Ⓓ

7 The total of the Sales day book had been calculated incorrectly. The correct total for sales was $11 200, but the total posted to the sales account was $12 100. The journal entry to correct the error is

(A) Dr Suspense $11 200   Cr Sales $11 200   Ⓐ

(B) Dr Sales $12 100   Cr Suspense $12 100   Ⓑ

(C) Dr Suspense $900   Cr Sales $900   Ⓒ

(D) Dr Sales $900   Cr Suspense $900   Ⓓ

7.5 Uses of the suspense account
7.6 Constructing suspense accounts

8 A suspense account was opened for an error of $300 found in the trial balance. Later it was discovered that purchases were understated by $300. The journal entry to correct this error is

(A) Dr Trading a/c   Cr Suspense a/c   Ⓐ

(B) Dr Suspense a/c   Cr Goods a/c   Ⓑ

(C) Dr Purchases a/c   Cr Suspense a/c   Ⓒ

(D) Dr Suspense a/c   Cr Purchases a/c   Ⓓ

7.7 Effects of errors on the income statement and balance sheet

9 The net profit of a firm was shown as $2 500 and it was later discovered that discounts received were undercast by $100 and purchases were understated by $150. What is the revised net profit?

(A) $2 450   Ⓐ

(B) $2 600   Ⓑ

(C) $2 550   Ⓒ

(D) $2 650   Ⓓ

10 The journals used to post entries in the Sales Ledger Control Account are

    I Sales Journal and Cash Book

    II Returns Inwards and General Journals

    III Returns Outwards and General Journals

(A) I   Ⓐ

(B) I and II   Ⓑ

(C) I and III   Ⓒ

(D) II and III   Ⓓ

11 Control accounts are prepared from totals taken from relevant books of original entry. Which of the following books of original entry totals would be used to prepare a Purchases Ledger Control Account?

    I General Journal

    II Purchases Day Book

    III Sales Day Book

(A) I   Ⓐ

(B) II   Ⓑ

(C) I and II   Ⓒ

(D) I and III   Ⓓ

12 From which of the following Books of Original Entry are contra entries between Sales Ledger Control Account and Purchases Ledger Control Account recorded?

(A) General Journal   Ⓐ

(B) Cash Book   Ⓑ

(C) Sales Day Book   Ⓒ

(D) Purchases Day Book   Ⓓ

13 Control accounts are very useful checking devices. They provide total trade receivables and trade payables. Which of the following ledgers contain individual personal accounts?

    I Sales ledger

    II Purchases ledger

    III General ledger

(A) I   (A)

(B) II   (B)

(C) I and II   (C)

(D) II and III   (D)

14 In which journal will interest charged by credit suppliers for overdue balances be posted?

(A) Purchases   (A)

(B) Cash Book   (B)

(C) Purchase Returns   (C)

(D) General Journal   (D)

<u>Item 15</u> refers to the following information provided by a trader.

	$
Debtors at the start of the year	10 000
Cash received from debtors during the year	25 000
Bad debts written off	500
Debtors at the end of the year	12 000

15 What was the amount of the trader's credit sales for the year?

(A) $22 500   Ⓐ

(B) $27 500   Ⓑ

(C) $35 000   Ⓒ

(D) $37 500   Ⓓ

<u>Item 16</u> refers to the following Purchases Ledger Control Account.

Purchases Ledger Control a/c					
2017		$	2017		$
Jun-30	Bank	30 000	Jun-01	Balance b/d	15 000
	Discount rec	2 000	30	Purchases	?
	Returns out	1 000			
	Balance c/d	5 000			
		38 000			**38 000**

16 What was the amount of purchases for the month of June?

(A) $5 000   Ⓐ

(B) $23 000   Ⓑ

(C) $30 000   Ⓒ

(D) $38 000   Ⓓ

Item 17 refers to the following information provided by Fitzroy Stephens.

2017		
May-1	Debtors Balance b/d	$30 000 (Dr)
31	Cash received from debtors during the year	$48 000
	Returns inwards	$3 000
	Discount allowed	$ 800
	Ending Debtors Balance	$8 000 (Cr)

17 What are the credit sales for the month of May?

(A) $8 000   Ⓐ

(B) $13 800   Ⓑ

(C) $30 000   Ⓒ

(D) $51 800   Ⓓ

18 Which of the following entries is NOT used to prepare the Purchases Ledger Control Account?

(A) Credit purchases   Ⓐ

(B) Debit balance on payables   Ⓑ

(C) Interest charged by a supplier   Ⓒ

(D) Interest charged to a customer for overdue accounts   Ⓓ

19 Which of the following should be entered in a sales ledger control account?

(A) Credit sales   Ⓐ

(B) Cash sales   Ⓑ

(C) Cost of sales   Ⓒ

(D) Discounts received   Ⓓ

20 A bank reconciliation statement shows the difference between the bank balance in a cash book of a business and the balance on a bank statement provided by a bank. Which of the following is shown as an item in the cash book and not on a bank statement?

(A) Credit transfers   (A)

(B) Bank charges   (B)

(C) Dishonoured cheques   (C)

(D) Unpresented cheques   (D)

21 Akowsa prepares her updated cash book on a monthly basis. Which of the following items will reduce Akowsa's current cash book balance?

    I Credit transfer

    II Bank charges

    III Standing order

(A) I   (A)

(B) II   (B)

(C) I and II   (C)

(D) II and III   (D)

Item 22 refers to the following information.

		Dr	Cr	Balance
2017		$	$	$
June-1	Balance b/f			260 (CR)
5	Deposit		1 000	
14	Standing order	50		
20	Credit transfer		40	
28	Bank charges	45		

22 The balance as per bank statement is

(A) Debit balance $1 205

(B) Credit balance $1 205

(C) Debit balance $1 300

(D) Credit balance $1 300

23 A firm's cash book showed a bank balance of $3 000. The bank statement showed bank charges of $50 and $80 for interest received. These amounts were not entered in the firm's cash book. What was the adjusted cash book balance?

(A) $2 970

(B) $3 000

(C) $3 030

(D) $3 130

Item 24 refers to the following information.

The bank columns of Donna's cash book showed a balance of $7 000 (credit). When Donna received the bank statement for the period, the following additional entries were made in the bank columns:

Bank charges	$600
Interest received	$1 600

24 What was the balance of the bank column (after updating the cash book)?

(A) $6 000 debit   (A)

(B) $6 000 credit   (B)

(C) $8 000 debit   (C)

(D) $8 000 credit   (D)

Item 25 refers to the following information.

Cheryl's cash book showed a balance of $4 740. The bank statement showed a different debit balance. Cheryl discovered that the following items were omitted:

Direct debit payment – water rates	$1 000
Bank charges	$100
Credit transfer	$2 000

25 What is the new cash book balance?

(A) $ 3 840   (A)

(B) $4 740   (B)

(C) $5 640   (C)

(D) $7 840   (D)

Section 8: Accounting for partnerships
8.1 Definition of a partnership

1 Which of the following partnership accounts are different from that of a sole trader?

    I Capital a/c

    II Current a/c

    III Appropriation a/c

(A) I only   Ⓐ

(B) I and II   Ⓑ

(C) I and III   Ⓒ

(D) II and III   Ⓓ

2 The form of business ownership in which there are at least two owners who share profits (losses) made by the business is known as a

(A) partnership.   Ⓐ

(B) proprietorship.   Ⓑ

(C) public limited company.   Ⓒ

(D) private limited company.   Ⓓ

3 Which of the following types of partners have unlimited liability?

    I General partners

    II Sleeping partners

    III Active partners

(A) I and II   Ⓐ

(B) I and III   Ⓑ

(C) II and III   Ⓒ

(D) I, II and III   Ⓓ

8.2 Features of a partnership

4 One of the features of a partnership is the willingness of parties to come together to form the partnership. What is this feature known as?

(**A**) Voluntary association   Ⓐ

(**B**) Mutual agency   Ⓑ

(**C**) Co-ownership of property   Ⓒ

(**D**) Unlimited liability   Ⓓ

8.3 Reasons for forming a partnership

5 Oscar is a sole trader who is considering forming a partnership with Gloria. Which of the following is NOT an advantage of forming this type of business?

(**A**) Combining skills   Ⓐ

(**B**) Increased capital   Ⓑ

(**C**) Greater specialization   Ⓒ

(**D**) Difficulty in decision making   Ⓓ

6 Maxwell and Thomas are two sole traders seeking to form a partnership. Which of the following are benefits of a forming a partnership?

    I Sharing of responsibilities

    II Sharing of risks

    III Increased capital

(**A**) I and II   Ⓐ

(**B**) I and III   Ⓑ

(**C**) II and III   Ⓒ

(**D**) I, II and III   Ⓓ

8.4 Components of a partnership agreement

7 What is the formal written agreement when a partnership is established known as?

(A) Partnership prospectus (A)

(B) Partnership deed (B)

(C) Memorandum of association (C)

(D) Certificate of incorporation (D)

8 In the absence of a partnership agreement, profits are shared

(A) equally. (A)

(B) in the agreed ratio. (B)

(C) in proportion to the capital invested. (C)

(D) to the partners who are actively involved in the business. (D)

8.5 The capital account of partners

9 Steve's Woodworking by Design is a sole trader who is forming a partnership with his brother Albert. Albert brings in equipment worth $15 000 and cash amounting to $3 000. How much capital did Albert invest into the partnership?

(A) $15 000 (A)

(B) $16 000 (B)

(C) $17 000 (C)

(D) $18 000 (D)

10 Plante and Rose are in partnership with a total investment of $45 000. Plante contributed equipment worth $5 000 and cash amounting to $10 000. How is Plante's contribution recorded in the journal?

(A)

Details	Dr	Cr
	$	$
Equipment	5 000	
Cash	10 000	
Capital		15 000

(A)

(B)

Details	Dr	Cr
	$	$
Capital	15 000	
Cash		10 000
Equipment		5 000

(B)

(C)

Details	Dr	Cr
	$	$
Capital	15 000	
Cash		15 000

(C)

(D)

Details	Dr	Cr
	$	$
Cash	15 000	
Capital		15 000

(D)

11 Adanna, Carla and Lystra are in partnership sharing profits and losses in the ratio 2:2:1 respectively. At the end of 2017 the partnership suffered a loss of $2 500. How much of this loss did Lystra incur?

(A) $250   (A)

(B) $500   (B)

(C) $1 000   (C)

(D) $1 500   (D)

Item 12 refers to the following information.

Crystal, Emerald, Jewel and Sapphire are in partnership sharing profits and losses in proportion to their capital. Their capitals are as follows:

Crystal	$4 000
Emerald	$5 000
Jewel	$2 000
Sapphire	$1 000

12 What is Jewel's share of profit of $15 000?

(A) $1 250   (A)

(B) $2 500   (B)

(C) $5 000   (C)

(D) $6 250   (D)

13 Kirell, Grell and Tyrell are in partnership sharing profits (losses) 2/5, 1/5 and 2/5 respectively. If the total profit is $16 000, what is each partner's residue of profit?

(A) Kirell $3 200, Grell $6 400, Tyrell $3 200   (A)

(B) Grell $6 400, Kirell $3 200, Tyrell $6 400   (B)

(C) Kirell $6 400, Grell $3 200, Tyrell $6 400   (C)

(D) Tyrell $3 200, Grell $6 400, Kirell $6 400   (D)

14 Which account shows how profits (losses) have been shared among partners?

(A) Current a/c   Ⓐ

(B) Capital a/c   Ⓑ

(C) Appropriation a/c   Ⓒ

(D) Profit and Loss a/c   Ⓓ

15 Karen and Wesley Williams are in partnership investing $45 500 and $50 000 respectively into the partnership. The partnership agreement states interest on capital is 5%. What is the total interest on capital to the partners?

(A) $2 275   Ⓐ

(B) $2 500   Ⓑ

(C) $4 577   Ⓒ

(D) $4 775   Ⓓ

16 Caleb and Joshua are in partnership sharing profits and losses in the ratio 2 : 3. From the information in the table below, what is the partnership's profit for the year?

	Caleb	Joshua
	$	$
Share of profit	2 400	3 600
Interest on capital	150	150
Salary	600	
Interest on drawings	60	100

(A) $6 000   Ⓐ

(B) $6 740   Ⓑ

(C) $6 900   Ⓒ

(D) $7 060   Ⓓ

Item 17 refers to the information in the following table.

Profit for the year*	$58 000
Salary: J. Singh	$ 5 000
Interest on capital	
C. Pierre	$2 500
J. Singh	$3 450
Interest on drawings	
C. Pierre	$ 100
J. Singh	$ 250
* profits are shared equally	

17 What will be each partner's share of profit?

(A) $23 350   Ⓐ

(B) $23 700   Ⓑ

(C) $29 000   Ⓒ

(D) $34 300   Ⓓ

8.8 The current account

18 Which of the following is shown in the current account but not in the appropriation account?

(A) Drawings   Ⓐ

(B) Interest on drawings   Ⓑ

(C) Interest on capital   Ⓒ

(D) Partners' salaries   Ⓓ

Items 19 and 20 refer to the following information.

Stevann, Karissa and D'neve are partners who share profits in the proportions of their capitals of $10 000, $20 000 and $30 000 respectively.

Net profit	$15 000
Interest on capital	5%
D'neve's salary	$4 000

19 Karissa's interest on capital is

(A) $500

(B) $1 000

(C) $1 500

(D) $3 000

(A)

(B)

(C)

(D)

20 What is the total appropriations for the partnership?

(A) $3 000

(B) $4 000

(C) $7 000

(D) $8 000

(A)

(B)

(C)

(D)

Items 21 and 22 refer to the following information.

Edward and Juanita started a partnership with fixed capitals of $75 000 and $100 000 respectively placed in the business's bank account. The following table provides information for the year ended 31 July 2015.

Current account balance:	
Edward	$5 000
Juanita	($1 500)
Drawings:	
Edward	$16 500
Juanita	$14 800
Profit	$80 000

The agreement states:

Profits and losses are shared 40% Edward; 60% Juanita.

Interest on capital is 10%.

Juanita is to receive a salary of $12 000.

21 What is the entry in the capital account?

(A) Dr Bank $175 000   Cr Capital: Edward $75 000, Juanita $100 000   Ⓐ

(B) Dr Capital: Edward 75 000, Juanita $100 000   Cr Bank $175 000   Ⓑ

(C) Dr Bank $430 000   Cr Capital: Edward $202 500, Juanita $227 500   Ⓒ

(D) Dr Capital: Edward $202 500, Juanita $227 500   Cr Bank $430 000   Ⓓ

22 What is Juanita's balance on her current a/c?

(A) Dr $20 500   Ⓐ

(B) Cr $20 500   Ⓑ

(C) Dr $53 700   Ⓒ

(D) Cr $53 700   Ⓓ

8.9 Debit and credit balances on the current account

<u>Items 23 and 24</u> refer to the following information.

On 1 August 2016, Brian had a debit balance on his current a/c of $3 000. At the end of the year he incurred interest on drawings of 5%: his drawings were $1 000. He obtained interest on capital of 5% on capital of $5 000, a salary $750 and shares of $4 500.

23 The current account balance on 1 August 2016 indicates that

(A) Brian owed the partnership. Ⓐ

(B) the partnership owed Brian. Ⓑ

(C) Brian's capital increased. Ⓒ

(D) Brian's capital decreased. Ⓓ

24 The balance on the current account on 1 August 2017 is

(A) Dr $1 450. Ⓐ

(B) Cr $1 450. Ⓑ

(C) Dr $5 500. Ⓒ

(D) Cr $5 500. Ⓓ

8.10 Treatment of current account balances in the balance sheet

25 A partner has a credit balance of $15 000. Interest on drawings is 10% of $11 000. The current account balance in the balance sheet at the end of the year is

(A) Dr $13 900. Ⓐ

(B) Cr $13 900. Ⓑ

(C) Dr $16 100. Ⓒ

(D) Cr $16 100. Ⓓ

1 Which organisation is established for charitable purposes?

(A) Cooperative (A)

(B) Non-profit organisation (B)

(C) Private limited liability company (C)

(D) Public limited liability company (D)

2 In which organisation are shares NOT transferable?

(A) Cooperative (A)

(B) Non-profit organisation (B)

(C) Private limited liability company (C)

(D) Public limited liability company (D)

3 The organisation in which owners do not possess shares is a

(A) Cooperative (A)

(B) Non-profit organisation (B)

(C) Private limited liability company (C)

(D) Public limited liability company (D)

4 Which organisation applies the principle of patronage refund?

(A) Cooperative (A)

(B) Non-profit organisation (B)

(C) Private limited liability company (C)

(D) Public limited liability company (D)

5 Liability is limited in which of the following organisations?

    I Cooperatives

    II Corporations

    III Partnerships

(A) I and II   Ⓐ

(B) I and III   Ⓑ

(C) II and III   Ⓒ

(D) I, II and III   Ⓓ

6 The principle of 'one man one vote' is an essential feature of which of the following?

    I Cooperatives

    II Corporations

    III Non-profit organisations

(A) I and II   Ⓐ

(B) I and III   Ⓑ

(C) II and III   Ⓒ

(D) I, II and III   Ⓓ

7 The organisation in which shares are ONLY transferable by the approval of the Board of Directors is a

(A) Cooperative   Ⓐ

(B) Non-profit organisation   Ⓑ

(C) Private limited liability company   Ⓒ

(D) Public limited liability company   Ⓓ

8 Helen is part of an organisation where the profits are never distributed to owners, regardless of the level of profit made, but are rather reinvested to assist its clients. This principle is applicable to which of the following?

(A) Cooperatives   Ⓐ

(B) Non-profit organisations   Ⓑ

(C) Private limited liability companies Ⓒ

(D) Public limited liability companies Ⓓ

9 For which organisation are shares sold/traded on the Stock Exchange?

(A) Partnership Ⓐ

(B) Non-profit organisation Ⓑ

(C) Private limited liability company Ⓒ

(D) Public limited liability company Ⓓ

10 A cooperative that seeks employment for its members is called which of the following?

(A) Agricultural cooperative Ⓐ

(B) Buyers cooperative Ⓑ

(C) Financial cooperative Ⓒ

(D) Workers cooperative Ⓓ

11 Joan Greaves belongs to a cooperative that grants loans to its members. This cooperative is which of the following?

(A) Agricultural cooperative Ⓐ

(B) Buyers cooperative Ⓑ

(C) Financial cooperative Ⓒ

(D) Workers cooperative Ⓓ

12 Castries Cricket Club, Kingston Children Orphanage and Grenada Teachers Trade Union are examples of which of the following?

(A) Cooperative Ⓐ

(B) Non-profit organisation Ⓑ

(C) Private limited liability company Ⓒ

(D) Public limited liability company Ⓓ

9.3 Advantages and disadvantages of a limited liability company

13 What advantage is common to a public limited liability company, a private limited liability company and a cooperative?

(A) Shares are easily transferable. Ⓐ

(B) They have limited liability. Ⓑ

(C) Friends and family are shareholders. Ⓒ

(D) No taxes are paid. Ⓓ

9.4 Methods of raising capital

14 A limited liability company raises equity by the issue of

    I Ordinary shares

    II Preference shares

    III Debentures

(A) I and II Ⓐ

(B) I and III Ⓑ

(C) II and III Ⓒ

(D) I, II and III Ⓓ

15 What are the other names for PAR VALUE?

    I Face value

    II Market value

    III Nominal value

(A) I and II Ⓐ

(B) I and III Ⓑ

(C) II and III Ⓒ

(D) I, II and III Ⓓ

16 A feature of private limited liability companies is that shares are

(A) not sold at all.   Ⓐ

(B) sold to members only.   Ⓑ

(C) sold on the stock exchange.   Ⓒ

(D) sold to family and friends.   Ⓓ

Items 17–19 refer to the following information.

Bridgetown Limited issues 3 000 ordinary shares (common stock) at $12 that has a par value of $10.

17 What is the DIFFERENCE between the par value of the share and the price that the share is sold for by Bridgetown Limited called?

(A) Nominal value   Ⓐ

(B) Share premium   Ⓑ

(C) Market value   Ⓒ

(D) Face value   Ⓓ

18 The total value ordinary shares to be recorded in the books of Bridgetown Limited is

(A) $6 000.   Ⓐ

(B) $30 000.   Ⓑ

(C) $33 000.   Ⓒ

(D) $36 000.   Ⓓ

19 Bridgetown Limited's share premium from the issue of the ordinary shares is

(A) $6 000.   Ⓐ

(B) $30 000.   Ⓑ

(C) $33 000.   Ⓒ

(D) $36 000.   Ⓓ

20 If Store Bay LLC receives a loan from Crown Point Bank Ltd, it has received

(A) equity capital. (A)

(B) debt capital. (B)

(C) revenue capital. (C)

(D) working capital. (D)

21 Debentures can be issued by a

(A) cooperative. (A)

(B) non-profit organisation. (B)

(C) private limited liability company. (C)

(D) public limited liability company. (D)

22 Debentures are

(A) loans sold to the public. (A)

(B) profits appropriated to shareholders. (B)

(C) shares sold to the public. (C)

(D) money donated to the business. (D)

9.5 Types of shares

23 Preference shares are shares held by shareholders who

(A) cannot transfer their shares. (A)

(B) are paid dividends before ordinary shareholders. (B)

(C) have more voting rights than ordinary shareholders. (C)

(D) sell their shares on the stock exchange before ordinary shareholders. (D)

Items 24 and 25 refer to the following information.

Lucian Enterprises Limited has 5 000 10% preference shares of $20 each. At the end of the financial period the business's net income was $32 000.

24 The 10% in front of preference shares means that these shareholders

    (A) pay 10% interest to the company.   Ⓐ

    (B) receive 10% interest from the company.   Ⓑ

    (C) receive 10% of the net income dividends.   Ⓒ

    (D) receive 10% of the value of their shares as dividends.   Ⓓ

25 The value of dividends paid to preference shareholders is

    (A) $500   Ⓐ

    (B) $3 200   Ⓑ

    (C) $10 000   Ⓒ

    (D) $100 000   Ⓓ

26 Which of the following statements is true about ordinary shareholders?

    (A) They bear the highest risk in the company   Ⓐ

    (B) They are not elected to the Board of Directors   Ⓑ

    (C) They have no voting rights at Annual General Meetings(AGMs) Ⓒ

    (D) They receive fixed dividends at the end of each year   Ⓓ

<u>Items 27–30</u> refer to the following information.

Amos Vale LLC in St. Vincent and Grenadines has been approved by the Registrar of Companies to have 200 000 $2 ordinary shares and 50 000 $4 10% preference shares. The company issued (sold) 40 000 ordinary shares at $2.50 each and 10 000 10% preference shares at $5.00 each. All the shares were fully subscribed.

27 Amos Vale Ltd's total authorised capital is

(A) $105 000. Ⓐ

(B) $150 000. Ⓑ

(C) $420 000. Ⓒ

(D) $600 000. Ⓓ

28 The journal to record the issue of preference shares is which of the following?

(A) Dr Cash $50 000   Cr Preference Shares $40 000, Share Premium $10 000 Ⓐ

(B) Dr Cash $50 000, Share Premium $10 000   Cr Preference Shares $40 000 Ⓑ

(C) Dr Preference Shares $50 000   Cr Cash $40 000, Share Premium $10 000 Ⓒ

(D) Dr Preference Shares $40 000, Share Premium $10 000   Cr Cash $10 000 Ⓓ

29 The journal entry to the issue (sale) of ordinary shares by Amos Vale LLC is

(A) Dr Cash $100 000   Cr Ordinary Shares $100 000 Ⓐ

(B) Dr Cash $100 000   Cr Ordinary Shares $80 000, Share Premium $20 000 Ⓑ

(C) Dr Ordinary Shares $100 000   Cr Cash $80 000, Share Premium $20 000 Ⓒ

(D) Dr Cash $100 000   Cr Ordinary Shares $100 000 Ⓓ

30 Amos Vale total share premium from the issue of both sets of shares is

(A) $10 000 Ⓐ

(B) $20 000 Ⓑ

(C) $30 000 Ⓒ

(D) $50 000 Ⓓ

31 Gingerland LLC located in Nevis does not want to increase the number of owners in the business. Which option is BEST suited for accomplishing this?

(A) Issue of debentures to the public   Ⓐ

(B) Issue of preference shares above par   Ⓑ

(C) Issue of preference shares to the public   Ⓒ

(D) Issue of ordinary shares at par to the public   Ⓓ

32 What are debentures classified as in the financial statements of a limited liability company?

(A) Assets   Ⓐ

(B) Revenue   Ⓑ

(C) Liabilities   Ⓒ

(D) Shareholders Equity   Ⓓ

Items 33 and 34 refer to the following information.

Saddlers LLC in St. Kitts issued 15 000 8% debentures at $20 each

33 What does the 8% represent?

(A) The interest to be received annually from debenture holders   Ⓐ

(B) The interest to be paid annually to debenture holders   Ⓑ

(C) The dividend to be paid annually by debentures holders   Ⓒ

(D) The dividend to be received annually by debenture holders   Ⓓ

34 The journal to record the issue of debentures by Saddlers LLC is

(A) Dr Cash $24 000   Cr Debentures $24 000   Ⓐ

(B) Dr Cash $276 000   Cr Debentures $276 000   Ⓑ

(C) Dr Cash $300 000   Cr Debentures $300 000   Ⓒ

(D) Dr Cash $324 000   Cr Debentures $324 000   Ⓓ

Items 35–38 refer to the following information.

St. Georges Enterprises started operations on 2 January 2017. At the end of the year they provided the following information.

	Authorised ($)	Issued ($)
Ordinary Shares ($4 par)	100 000	70 000
8% Preference Shares ($5 par)	50 000	30 000
6% Debentures		50 000

Dividends to be paid to ordinary shareholders – 30%

Net Income for the year - $60 000

35 Which group of persons represents the order in which payments should be made by the company, that is, first, second and third?

(A) Debenture holders, preference shareholders, ordinary shareholders   (A)

(B) Preference shareholders, debenture holders, ordinary shareholders   (B)

(C) Ordinary shareholders, preference shareholders, debenture holders   (C)

(D) Debenture holders, ordinary shareholders, preference shareholders   (D)

36 What is the total payment of dividends to ordinary shareholders?

(A) $3 000   (A)

(B) $4 000   (B)

(C) $18 000   (C)

(D) $21 000   (D)

37 What is the total interest payment to debenture holders?

(A) $600   (A)

(B) $3 000   (B)

(C) $3 600   (C)

(D) $10 000   (D)

38 What is the total dividend payment to preference shareholders?

(A) $2 400   Ⓐ

(B) $4 000   Ⓑ

(C) $4 800   Ⓒ

(D) $6 000   Ⓓ

9.8 Appropriation of profits between dividends and reserves

Items 39–41 refer to the following information.

Dennery Private Limited Company (PLC) of St. Lucia supplied the following information at the end of 2018.

Net income for the year	$70 000
Retained profits b/f 01/01/18	$20 000
Ordinary shares ($2 par)	$120 000
Ordinary dividend	$0.50 per share
6% Preference dividend ($5 par)	$90 000

The Board of Directors of Dennery PLC agreed to transfer $5 000 to the general reserve and $6 000 to the training reserve.

39 Total value of profits available before appropriations of dividends and transfers is

(A) $20 000.   Ⓐ

(B) $50 000.   Ⓑ

(C) $70 000.   Ⓒ

(D) $90 000.   Ⓓ

40 Total profits available after transfer to reserves is

(A) $9 000.   Ⓐ

(B) $39 000.   Ⓑ

(C) $59 000.   Ⓒ

(D) $79 000.   Ⓓ

41 Total profits available to ordinary shareholders is

(A) $33 500.   Ⓐ

(B) $73 600.   Ⓑ

(C) $84 400.   Ⓒ

(D) $95 600.   Ⓓ

9.9 Final accounts of limited liability companies and co-operatives

42 In the Balance Sheet, dividends not yet paid are classified under

(A) Current Assets.   Ⓐ

(B) Non-current Assets.   Ⓑ

(C) Current Liabilities.   Ⓒ

(D) Non-current Liabilities.   Ⓓ

43 In the financial statements of which type of business are profits referred to as surplus?

I Limited liability company

II Cooperative

III Non-profit organisation

(A) I and II   Ⓐ

(B) I and III   Ⓑ

(C) II and III   Ⓒ

(D) I, II and III   Ⓓ

44 Which of the following organisations has a Shareholders' Equity section in its financial statements?

      I Limited liability company

      II Cooperative

      III Non-profit organisation

(A) I and II   Ⓐ

(B) I and III   Ⓑ

(C) II and III   Ⓒ

(D) I, II and III   Ⓓ

45 In a cooperative, Patronage Refund is recorded as which of the following?

(A) Equity in the Balance Sheet   Ⓐ

(B) A current asset in the Balance Sheet   Ⓑ

(C) An expense in the Income Statement   Ⓒ

(D) An appropriation in the Appropriation Account   Ⓓ

Items 46–48 refer to the following information.

The ratios of four limited liability companies from Belize have been provided in the following table.

Name of Company	Punta Gorda PLC	Hopkins Ltd	San Ignacio Ltd	Dangriga Inc.
Current Ratio	2.5 : 1	1.67 : 1	2.51 : 1	1.76 : 1
Acid Test	1.89 : 1	0.89 : 1	1.99 : 1	0.99 : 1
Inventory Turnover	11 times	7 times	13 times	9 times
Gross Profit Percentage	50%	42%	57%	48%
Net Profit Percentage	17%	11%	15%	13%

46 Which company has the strongest liquidity position?

(A) Dangriga Inc.

(B) Hopkins Ltd

(C) Punta Gorda PLC

(D) San Ignacio Ltd

Ⓐ

Ⓑ

Ⓒ

Ⓓ

47 Which company is the second slowest in selling its inventory?

(A) Dangriga Inc.

(B) Hopkins Ltd

(C) Punta Gorda PLC

(D) San Ignacio Ltd

Ⓐ

Ⓑ

Ⓒ

Ⓓ

48 Which company had the highest financial performance after expenses?

(A) Dangriga Inc.

(B) Hopkins Ltd

(C) Punta Gorda PLC

(D) San Ignacio Ltd

Ⓐ

Ⓑ

Ⓒ

Ⓓ

49 Paul Binge donated $10 000 to the Children's Charitable Fund. This donation was recorded

(A) as a current liability in its Balance Sheet. (A)

(B) as an expense in the Income and Expenditure Statement. (B)

(C) on the Cr Side of the Receipts and Payments Account. (C)

(D) on the Dr Side of the Receipts and Payments Account. (D)

50 A subscription paid to a non-profit organisation is recorded as

(A) expenditure. (A)

(B) liabilities. (B)

(C) payments. (C)

(D) receipts. (D)

Section 10: Manufacturing and inventory control
10.1 Elements of cost

1 How are royalties classified in a manufacturing firm?

(A) Direct expense (A)

(B) Indirect expense (B)

(C) Administrative expense (C)

(D) Selling and distribution expense (D)

Factory workers wages	$2 250
Direct materials	$3 200
Factory lighting	$550
Factory manager's salary	$2 400
Indirect materials	$625

2 What is the total value of direct expenses?

(A) $3 200   Ⓐ

(B) $5 200   Ⓑ

(C) $5 450   Ⓒ

(D) $9 025   Ⓓ

3 What is the total value of indirect expenses?

(A) $625   Ⓐ

(B) $2 950   Ⓑ

(C) $3 025   Ⓒ

(D) $3 575   Ⓓ

10.2 Preparation of manufacturing accounts

4 Which of the following is NOT an example of a manufacturing firm?

(A) Grocery   Ⓐ

(B) Bakery   Ⓑ

(C) Garment factory   Ⓒ

(D) Woodworking shop   Ⓓ

5 Total production cost is equal to

(A) Prime Cost + Factory Overheads.   Ⓐ

(B) Prime Cost – Factory Overheads.   Ⓑ

(C) Factory Overheads + Selling and Distribution Expenses.   Ⓒ

(D) Selling and Distribution Expenses + Prime Cost.   Ⓓ

Item 6 refers to the following information.

Stock of raw materials at start	$1 200
Direct labour	$3 000
Stock of raw materials at end	$1 500
Factory overheads	$7 500
Stock of work-in-progress at start	$800
Purchases of raw materials	$2 000
Stock of work-in-progress at end	$1 000

6 The total cost of goods produced is

(A) $12 000.   Ⓐ

(B) $12 400.   Ⓑ

(C) $14 500.   Ⓒ

(D) $17 000.   Ⓓ

Item 7 refers to the following information.

Stock of raw materials at start	$250
Purchases of raw materials	$875
Stock of raw materials at end	$200
Freight on raw materials	$125

7 The cost of raw materials consumed is

(A) $800.   Ⓐ

(B) $1 050.   Ⓑ

(C) $1 125.   Ⓒ

(D) $1 450.   Ⓓ

8 If 250 units were produced at a cost of $30 000 and transferred to the Trading Account at a 5% mark up, what is the unit cost of production?

(A) $6   Ⓐ

(B) $114   Ⓑ

(C) $120   Ⓒ

(D) $126   Ⓓ

10.4 Preparation of final accounts for a manufacturing concern

9 Which section of the Balance Sheet of a manufacturing firm is most likely to differ from the Balance Sheet of a retail firm?

(A) Owner's Equity   Ⓐ

(B) Current Assets   Ⓑ

(C) Current Liabilities   Ⓒ

(D) Non-current Assets   Ⓓ

10 A business had opening stock of finished goods of $55 000, cost of goods produced $120 000, sales $150 000 and closing stock of finished goods $75 000. What is the Gross Profit?

(A) $20 000   Ⓐ

(B) $30 000   Ⓑ

(C) $50 000   Ⓒ

(D) $100 000   Ⓓ

11 The total cost of producing 100 tables is $12 000 and a mark-up of 20% per unit is added. What is price per table using the mark-up pricing method?

(A) $24   Ⓐ

(B) $96   Ⓑ

(C) $120   Ⓒ

(D) $144   Ⓓ

10.6 Methods of inventory valuation

12 Which of the following are methods of inventory valuation?

    I First In Last Out

    II Average Cost

    III Last In First Out

(A) I and II   Ⓐ

(B) I and III   Ⓑ

(C) II and III   Ⓒ

(D) I, II and III   Ⓓ

10.7 Calculation of the value of closing inventory

Items 13 and 14 refer to the following options.

    I Issues

    II Receipts

    III Balance of stock

13 Which of the above information from a stock card appears in a Trading Account?

(A) I and II only   Ⓐ

(B) I and III only   Ⓑ

(C) II and III only   Ⓒ

(D) I, II and III   Ⓓ

14 Which of the above information from a stock card appears in a Balance Sheet?

(A) III only   Ⓐ

(B) I and II only   Ⓑ

(C) I and III only   Ⓒ

(D) II and III only   Ⓓ

<u>Items 15–20</u> refer to the following information.

Receipts	
1 May	20 units at $4 each
3 May	40 units at $5 each
6 May	60 units at $6 each
Issued	
5 May	25 units at $7 each
7 May	40 units at $8 each
8 May	30 units at $8 each

15 The total value of purchases is

(A) $360.   Ⓐ

(B) $480.   Ⓑ

(C) $600.   Ⓒ

(D) $640.   Ⓓ

16 The total value of sales is

(A) $240.   Ⓐ

(B) $665.   Ⓑ

(C) $735.   Ⓒ

(D) $760.   Ⓓ

17 Using the First In First Out Method, closing inventory would be valued at

(A) $95.   Ⓐ

(B) $105.   Ⓑ

(C) $125.   Ⓒ

(D) $150.   Ⓓ

18 Using the Last In First Out Method, closing inventory would be valued at

(A) $95   Ⓐ

(B) $105   Ⓑ

(C) $125   Ⓒ

(D) $150   Ⓓ

19 What would be the gross profit using the First In First Out Method?

(A) $200   Ⓐ

(B) $245   Ⓑ

(C) $1 225   Ⓒ

(D) $1 235   Ⓓ

20 What is the average cost of inventory on hand at 3 May?

(A) $4.33   Ⓐ

(B) $4.50   Ⓑ

(C) $4.67   Ⓒ

(D) $6.67   Ⓓ

Section 11: Accounting for the entrepreneur
11.1 Methods of payment

1 Which of the following is the LEAST likely method of payment for employees' wages?

(A) Cash   Ⓐ

(B) Cheque   Ⓑ

(C) Direct deposit   Ⓒ

(D) Electronic fund transfer at point of sale (EFTPOS)   Ⓓ

2 Mr. Robert purchased equipment from Belview Ltd. What is the LEAST likely method of payment?

(A) Cash   Ⓐ

(B) Cheque   Ⓑ

(C) Direct Deposit   Ⓒ

(D) Electronic fund transfer at point of sale (EFTPOS)   Ⓓ

11.2 Source documents of the payroll
11.3 Preparation of payroll and wage documents

3 Which of the following source documents are NOT used when recording payroll?

(A) Invoices   Ⓐ

(B) Time cards   Ⓑ

(C) Electronic clock in cards   Ⓒ

(D) Employee earnings record cards   Ⓓ

4 The records that can be drawn up from the completed paysheet are

      I electronic clock in card.

      II employee earnings record.

      III pay slip.

(A) I and II   Ⓐ

(B) I and III   Ⓑ

(C) II and III   Ⓒ

(D) I, II and III   Ⓓ

11.4 Main accounting software used for payroll

5 Which of the following software will NOT be used for payroll?

(A) Paymaster Payroll Solutions   Ⓐ

(B) Peachtree Accounting   Ⓑ

(C) Microsoft publisher   Ⓒ

(D) QuickBooks   Ⓓ

11.5 Statutory and voluntary/non-statutory deductions

6 Which of the following are considered statutory deductions?

      I Income tax

      II National Insurance

      III Life Insurance

(A) I and II   Ⓐ

(B) I and III   Ⓑ

(C) II and III   Ⓒ

(D) I, II and III   Ⓓ

7 Which of the following are NOT non-statutory deductions?

(A) Savings plan (A)

(B) Trade union dues (B)

(C) Insurance premium (C)

(D) Social Security contributions (D)

11.6 Calculation of employees' earnings

8 When pay is based on the amount of work done or the number of units produced, this is known as which of the following?

(A) Commission (A)

(B) Fixed rates (B)

(C) Piece rates (C)

(D) Time rates (D)

9 Zachary works in a factory. He is paid $5.00 for each finished product that has completed the quality check. The company's wage agreement states that Zachary is entitled to a minimum of $1 000 per week. During the week ending 15 July, Zachary completed 200 items of which 20 items were rejected. What is Zachary's pay for the week?

(A) $900 (A)

(B) $1 000 (B)

(C) $1 090 (C)

(D) $1 100 (D)

Item 10 refers to the following information.

Deductions are made from the gross salary of Ms. Karyn Grace as shown in the table.

Deductions
Income tax – 25%
National Insurance – 3%
Credit Union Contributions – $300

10 What is the value of total deductions from Ms. Grace's gross salary of $2 000 per month?

(A) $300   Ⓐ

(B) $560   Ⓑ

(C) $860   Ⓒ

(D) $1 140   Ⓓ

Item 11 refers to the following information.

The weekly wage agreement for production workers for The Sweet Tooth factory is as shown in the following table.

$30 per hour for a 40 hr week
Double time excess of 40 hrs
Triple time for hours worked on Saturday, Sunday or Public Holidays

11 For the week, Randee worked 50 hours in addition to 4 hours on Saturday and 3 hours on Sunday. His gross wage is

(A) $1 200.   Ⓐ

(B) $1 230.   Ⓑ

(C) $2 400.   Ⓒ

(D) $2 430.   Ⓓ

Items 12–14 refer to the information in the following table.

Payroll Records of La Pierre Service Station – week ending 28 July 2017								
						Deductions		
Employee	Position	Hourly Rate	Regular Hrs	Overtime hours *	Income tax	National Insurance	Union Dues	Life Insurance
		$	No. of hrs.	No. of hrs.	Rate	$	$	$
Danielle Williams	Manager	30	40	10	10%	2%	20	80
Shalome Ferdinand	Supervisor	20	40	5	10%	2%	20	20
Savion McIntosh	Attendant	10	40	0	10%	2%	20	10

* Note: Overtime is paid time-and–a-half for more than 40 hours per week.

12 The net wages for the manager for this period are

(A) $1 352. Ⓐ

(B) $1 500. Ⓑ

(C) $1 650. Ⓒ

(D) $1 948. Ⓓ

13 The total of deductions for Shalomé Ferdinand are

(A) $116. Ⓐ

(B) $128. Ⓑ

(C) $134. Ⓒ

(D) $154. Ⓓ

14 The net wages of the three employees totals

(A) $2 400. Ⓐ

(B) $2 470. Ⓑ

(C) $2 740. Ⓒ

(D) $3 000. Ⓓ

15 In 2019 Michele received a yearly salary of $150 000. In 2020, she will receive a yearly pay increase of 3%. At 31 December 2020, Michele's monthly salary is

(A) $12 500. (A)

(B) $12 875. (B)

(C) $15 000. (C)

(D) $15 450. (D)

Item 16 refers to the following information about an employee D. Dowlath.

Net Pay	$8 125
Income Tax	$1 625
National Insurance	$60
Health Contribution	$20

16 What is D. Dowlath's gross pay?

(A) $4 620 (A)

(B) $6 420 (B)

(C) $8 930 (C)

(D) $9 830 (D)

11.7 Preparation of simple cash flow projection and outflow

17 A cash budget is a summary of expected

    I receipts.

    II payments.

    III units to be produced for sales.

(A) I (A)

(B) II (B)

(C) I and II (C)

(D) I and III (D)

18 Which of the following items would NOT be included in the preparation of a cash flow (cash budget)?

    I Depreciation

    II Capital invested (owner's equity)

    III Provision for bad debts

(A) I   Ⓐ

(B) II   Ⓑ

(C) I and II   Ⓒ

(D) I and III   Ⓓ

19 Which of the following are reasons for the preparation of a cash budget?

    I Forecasting receipts and payments

    II Forecasting sales

    III Reflecting cash surpluses and cash shortages

(A) I   Ⓐ

(B) II   Ⓑ

(C) I and II   Ⓒ

(D) I and III   Ⓓ

Items 20 and 21 relate to the following information.

Sherma is planning to start her own company. She intends to open a bank account with $20 000. One of the staff from a micro lending agency assisted her in preparing a cash budget. The budget contained the following information for the first three months of her business.

	June	July	August
	$	$	$
Opening balance	Nil	?	5 000
Add: Receipts			
Capital invested	20 000		
Sales	Nil	5 000	7 000
Total cash available	20 000	18 000	12 000
Less: Payments			
Utilities	2 000	3 000	3 000
Salaries and wages	5 000	10 000	10 000
Total cash payments	7 000	13 000	13 000
Closing balance	13 000	5 000	?

20 What is the opening expected balance for the beginning of July?

(A) Nil   Ⓐ

(B) $7 000 deficit   Ⓑ

(C) $13 000 surplus   Ⓒ

(D) $20 000 surplus   Ⓓ

21 What is the closing expected balance for the month of August?

(A) $1 000 surplus   Ⓐ

(B) $1 000 deficit   Ⓑ

(C) $5 000 surplus   Ⓒ

(D) $5 000 deficit   Ⓓ

11.8 Preparation of simple sales and production budgets

Item 22 refers to the following information.

Harold disclosed the sales information in the following table.

Month	Sales Units
May	20 000
June	40 000
July	70 000

His company has 5 000 units on hand on 1 May. Assume that Harold Company requires an ending inventory to 25% of the following month of sales.

22 The total number of units Harold Company needs to produce for the month of June is

(A) 10 000.   Ⓐ

(B) 17 500.   Ⓑ

(C) 47 500.   Ⓒ

(D) 57 500.   Ⓓ

23 Which of the following statements is NOT correct?

(A) A sales budget predicts future dollars of sales.   (A)

(B) A sales budget is prepared after the cash budget.   (B)

(C) A sales budget indicates the expected selling price of each unit.   (C)

(D) A sales budget is prepared before the production budget.   (D)

24 A sales target is the

    I projection of potential sales for an industry.

    II estimate of expected sales for a budgeted period.

    III estimate of a company's expected share of sales.

(A) I   (A)

(B) II   (B)

(C) I and II   (C)

(D) II and III   (D)

25 Which of the following budgets show expected unit of sales?

(A) Cash   (A)

(B) Sales   (B)

(C) Purchases   (C)

(D) Production   (D)

26 Which of the following budgets shows the expected number of units to be produced?

(A) Cash   (A)

(B) Sales   (B)

(C) Purchases   (C)

(D) Production   (D)

Item 27 refers to the following information.

The selling price of a company's product is $100 per unit. The company has estimated sales in units for the period April to June as follows.

Months	April	May	June
Units	700	800	750

27 How much is the total anticipated sales for the period?

(A) $70 000

(B) $75 000

(C) $80 000

(D) $225 000

Ⓐ

Ⓑ

Ⓒ

Ⓓ

11.9 Preparation of a simple business plan

28 A business plan

    I shows how resources will be used.

    II identifies when to start a business.

    III outlines how profits will be generated.

(A) I

(B) II

(C) I and II

(D) I and III

Ⓐ

Ⓑ

Ⓒ

Ⓓ